FAREWELL, MY YOUTH

Farewell, My Youth

BY
ARNOLD BAX

GREENWOOD PRESS, PUBLISHERS
WESTPORT, CONNECTICUT

Many of my friends whose names appear in the following pages are no longer in our world. To their loved memory I dedicate this little book.

Originally published in 1943
by Longmans, Green and Company, London

First Greenwood Reprinting 1970

Library of Congress Catalogue Card Number 78-100221

SBN 8371-3246-0

Printed in the United States of America

FOREWORD

What shall I do with this absurdity—
O heart, O troubled heart—this caricature.
Decrepit age that has been tied to me
As to a dog's tail?

W. B. YEATS.

MY HARD CURSE UPON INCREASING AGE

Well, I have not reached so desolate a pass as yet, but only the other day my brother Clifford agreed with me that there are no compensations to weigh against advancing years—no, not one!

Speaking for myself alone I am decidedly no wiser than I was at twenty-five, and anyhow would I not prefer to be young and harum-scarum than an elderly Solon?

Am I any more at peace with myself and with the world at large than I was in my 'teens? As I shall tell later, I once found a queer peace in a Bohemian pine-forest at twenty-three and under exceptional and irrecoverable circumstances, but on the whole I am inclined to answer: No, and I am not at all sure that I really desire the sort of peace of which you are probably thinking. It has always seemed to me rather dull.

And then the tragi-comedy of the body!

I resent the buzzing of blood in my temples whenever I stoop to tie a shoelace or pick up my pen from the floor; the thickening of tissue beneath the skin in front of my ears and under my chin; the degrading fact that in order to rise from any deep arm-chair I needs must huddle my trunk forward and lever myself up by pressing hard upon the arms.

I deplore the recession of hair from my brow and amplifying waist-line. (I am in no way ambitious to be approved by Julius Caesar.) When I am addressed as "sir" by lithe and hirsute young men I fall into despondency, and the increasing courtesy of police-men,[1] porters, booking-office clerks, and lavatory attendants is a

---

[1] Arnold Bennett once remarked that his earliest recognition of his own middle age came at a certain appalling moment when he realized for the first time that the policeman at the corner was a mere youth.

6   FOREWORD

cause of panic. If I live to be seventy I shall celebrate that birthday by abusing old age with a malevolence even more savage than that evinced by Yeats in the bitter and splendid poem I have quoted.

Rudeness from one's elders (but not necessarily betters) seems to proffer a kind of certificate of one's youth. Beginning with the barbarous insults heaped upon schoolboys by ushers, and proceeding to the gratuitous offensiveness of Birmingham bagmen to young artists in Dublin commercial hotels (I knew about this one), we pass to insolence in full riotous bloom from the president of an Army Medical Board at Reading Barracks during the Great War. And then after one turns thirty or so, youth itself and the tide of boorishness are found, imperceptibly at first, to be receding. And so it goes on, sad indeed, with no solace anywhere. But stay, I discern one grain of comfort which I stoop (wheezily) to gather up. Post-office girls are, with very few exceptions, as offhand and sullen in manner as ever they were. So there remains a chance that actual senility may be deferred for a time yet, and whilst I retain a modicum of my faculties and still contrive immunity from elephantiasis, beri-beri, and Addison's disease, I will try to set down a few memories for the entertainment (and possibly warning) of my friends.

Morar,
Inverness-shire.

FAREWELL, MY YOUTH

OVER THE THRESHOLD

Diffidently I ventured into this world (as I am happy now to say, for I would not have missed it) by way of Streatham in the County of Surrey. Be it noted that this statement may be taken as official. I say this because there have been divergent schools of thought regarding the event.

I have been informed (in print) that I was born on an island in the middle of a bog-lake in County Mayo. It has also been asserted that I am a "spoiled priest," as the Irish call one who has studied for Holy Orders and has later abandoned the career on discovery of a lack of vocation. And did not George Russell ("Æ") once send me a cutting from the Dublin *Freeman's Journal* (now long defunct) proclaiming that "Arnold Bax" was a pseudonym, adopted solely for musical purposes, by a West of Ireland poet and novelist named Dermot O'Byrne? (Well, there was some small excuse for this as will be shown later.) These fantasies are picturesque, but unfortunately not true, and though those fellows may have been right, and I had come to the wrong place, I reaffirm that I was born uninterestingly—except perhaps to my mother and myself—at Streatham in the County of Surrey, at 8.30 in the morning of November 8th, 1883.

In a physical sense there is a certain appropriateness about this location of my début since we Baxes come of an old Surrey stock. Amongst the earliest followers of Penn the Quaker, members of the family owned many lands, manors, cottages, farms, fiefs, and messuages in the county from the sixteenth to the eighteenth century. These were for the greater part situated within a rough circle, of which the road between Dorking and Horsham forms the diameter. A direct ancestor held Kitlands near Coldharbour, Leith Hill, in 1624, and his grandson bought Ockley Court in 1692, and (I reflect upon this fact with a certain fat and snobbish complacency) was for a short time Lord of the Manor.

Yes, I am proud of this, my forebears' lovely village, said by many to be the prettiest in Surrey.

Yet, all the same, I am never certain that I ought not to have been born on that island in the Connaught bog-lake.

STREATHAM

I cherish a fancy—or delusion—that Streatham in the 'eighties was still Surrey, and not yet just S.W.—whatever it may be. Memories intruding from early childhood suggest that architecturally it was a little better than its neighbours, Clapham, frankly and rowdily vulgar, and Balham—the Wigan of the south—now a stale music-hall joke. Hazily do I recall a certain mellowness and port-wininess about some of the older streets of my birthplace, an atmosphere which even now makes Richmond the pleasantest place hard by London. Kenmure, the last grandfatherly residence, was a small but dignified house, standing back from the street in a reserved manner behind a high brick wall. There was a short glass-covered passage leading from the outer wrought-iron gate to the front door, and in my youthful opinion this lent great distinction to the whole place.

I do not know why, but I always associate Streatham with the fall of the year, for I picture it with bluish mist amongst the thinning garden trees, and large deciduously golden horse-chestnut leaves sprawling in the damp underfoot. Maybe I never saw it in any livelier season.

That extraordinarily restless man, my paternal grandfather, died before my time. As I said just now, Kenmure was the last of his innumerable domiciles. He never contrived to stay in any one house longer than about six months, though why I cannot say, for I have never learned the reason for his will-o'-the-wisp habits.

I cannot entertain the idea (though it would be fun!) that he was ever particularly wanted by the police, nor do I imagine that he was hag-ridden by dread of the hot breath of questing tradesmen creditors upon the back of his neck. Probably he was the victim of that vague anxiety-neurosis which is a rather marked defect in my family. We can face up well enough to known ills and dangers, but we are apt to dither in imagination of the hidden assailant; unsubstantial phantom though he may turn out to be.

The Borough of Streatham has now doubtless caught the common infection of the suburbs, and pullulates with gaudy petrol-pumps and super-gorgeous cinema-houses. I should be glad to think that I am wrong, and that I am calumniating a town-planner's masterpiece. To tell truth, the place has not been revisited since my brother and I, as small boys, were privileged to play our first cricket with a reputedly brilliant young Oxonian named John Simon, later to come more or less prominently before the eye of the public (and still more recently into its pocket). Oh yes, I like to dream that the erectors of modern Streatham have built Jerusalem in England's green and pleasant land, but I am much afraid that in any wide-awake moment I should stake my last shirt on the petrol-pumps.

ROMANTICISM

I distinctly remember my first conscious apprehension of beauty. It may have been in 1889. Whilst staying with my parents in Worthing I was taken one September evening to the top of Arundel Park. It was the hour of sunset, and as we stood there an unimaginable glory of flame developed in the west so that all the wooded heights seemed on fire. Even the east was stained with pale coral. It might have been Ragnarök, the burning of the Gods in Norse mythology. I watched speechlessly. To my childish perception this visitation was sheer all-conquering splendour and majesty, untroubled by the sense of the transitoriness of all lovely things. The hour was immortal.

That all-too-early sorrow for the mutability of all things was revealed to me, I think, in the following year. We had been in Ockley all a long golden day of summer, and whilst we were returning to Victoria in the train, the sunset, at first a magnificence of tranquil bands of crimson and gold, gradually smouldered dimmer and duller behind Leith Hill with its tower and pine-trees. And suddenly an ache of regret that this particular day of beauty should come to an end and nevermore return wrung my heart so cruelly that, unseen, I wept bitterly in my shadowy corner of the carriage.

> Its edges foamed with amethyst and rose
> Withers once more the old blue flower of day.
> There where the ether like a diamond glows
> Its petals fade away.

> Brightness falls from the air;
> Queens have died young and fair;
> Dust hath closéd Helen's eye.

This tenderness of pain, half cruel, half sweet, is surely an essential quality of the never clearly defined "Romantic mood."

MY PARENTS

On my arrival on this plane (as some "ist"—I forget which—might express it) I found myself confronted with a fierce old paternal grandmother, a very eager and inquiring young mother, and a somewhat remote father with whom I never became really intimate. He was nearly forty when I was born, and I cannot recall him otherwise than as an elderly man. His was a timid and unobtrusive personality, though in character he was firm enough where his rigid—almost Calvinistic—principles were at stake. For instance, nothing would induce him to enter a theatre, since he had been brought up by his stern-lipped mother to look upon such places of entertainment as boiling vats of moral evil—antechambers of hell. I do not think that children came naturally into his line of country, for he never had much to say to us, nor we to him. I still picture him, perched upon the highest stool I ever saw—an affair of black wood with a blue plush seat which he achieved by means of a step-ladder—absorbed in copying out details from parish registers which he had patiently collected, or recording notes concerning the past of our family painstakingly compiled by him over a long period of years. These and archaeological matters of all kinds were his enthusiasms.

A Fellow of the Society of Antiquaries ("The Antics" as my mother frivolously bynamed it) he cared for little that was less than a century old, and almost anything older than that. A romantic in his way, and a true dyed-in-the-wool escapologist if there ever was one.

He was fond of music (choral music especially), but warned my brother—in the latter's earlier and more eccentric phase as a poet in life as well as in letters—that verse was merely "rich pastry." "You can't live on it, my boy!" And long after that day, should Clifford or I find the other, pen in hand and paper before him, the query always came, "Rolling pastry again?" or even "Rolling?" *tout court.*

My father was entirely under the sway of his mother, that spartan

matron, and when her empire fell with her death in 1890 he was
ruled by his young wife, something of a despot too, but of a far
more benevolent type.

My mother, seventeen years my father's junior, was, as I first
remember her, a lively, restless, pretty young woman, socially alert,
her hand ever in her purse to help the needy, both deserving and
undeserving, for her impulsiveness and natural gift of sympathy
made her an easy dupe, and in her old age still did so. Loving
admiration, perhaps over-sensitive, quick-tempered, and quick to
forgive, delighting in the vigorous management of people and affairs,
she was a live wire indeed in the extremely dull society in which
her early married days were spent. I have always said that she would
have made a very good queen. All her life intensely religious, she
was, for a Victorian, unusually tolerant of the beliefs of others.
Her own convictions were for long very unstable, and from time
to time she must have examined the credentials of most of the forms
of Christianity, and even stepped outside to take a glance at Dr.
R. J. Campbell's new theology, and theosophy. Finally she reached
the end of her varied and curious spiritual wanderings in the quiet
haven of the Church of Rome.

FIRST MUSIC

Now I do not propose to be tiresome about my early childhood.
Other people's infancy and the years immediately following can
only amuse psycho-analysts, and they are often far more interested
in the subject than is right or proper. I pass over six or seven years
in merciful silence, only pausing to mention that during that period
three more children were born to my parents—Aubrey, a radiant
and enterprising lad, who died at ten years of meningitis: Clifford,
the poet and dramatist: and my sister Evelyn.

I cannot remember a time when I had not the same miserable
smattering of French which is all I can muster now, and similarly
I cannot recall the long-lost day when I was unable to play the
piano—inaccurately.

It seems that I could always read printed music at the piano-stool
with the same unthinking ease with which a man reads a book.
I claim no merit in this. It is merely a natural gift, like thick hair or

strong teeth. I improved my playing and sight-reading with the assistance of an ancient, foxed, and yellowing edition of Beethoven's symphonies, arranged for piano solo. These and the sonatas I played for several years, all day long; just as later on I performed Wagner's music dramas all day and parts of the night for years. And yet there were no complaints from the heroic family!

My earliest distant acquaintance with the orchestra came when I was taken for the first time to one of the Crystal Palace Saturday Concerts. My father had been a subscriber since 1860, and unfailing attendance at "the Palace" every Saturday afternoon was for him a religious observance almost comparable with the obligation laid upon the devout Catholic to hear Holy Mass every Sunday (I fear my Puritan father would scarcely have relished this sentence!).

He had kept every analytical programme from the beginning of his concert-going career, and there they were in the dining-room bookcase, neatly bound year by year in fat black volumes. Intensely interesting it was to observe names, afterwards to become eminent, creeping stealthily into those old, old programmes.

M. P. Tschaikowsky's piano concerto in B flat, played for the first time in England by Edward Dannreuter in 1877, with some account of that entirely unknown young Russian composer; as an appendix to one programme specimen quotations from Herr Brahms' new symphony in D, "to be performed later in the season, it was hoped, if the parts were available." And of course the furiously discussed Richard Wagner, trampling into our musical life with Nazi-like insistence.

I used to spend hours over these volumes, amusing myself by improvising absurd symphonies and overtures from the musical excerpts.

The orchestral playing at that time must, I am sure, have been pretty rough; for example, there was no unanimity of phrasing amongst the strings, each player bowing according to his individual fancy, and the notes of the horn were often all too liquid.

I used to sit in vast and delicious awe of the conductor, August Manns, who by the way always appeared in white kid gloves, and with a white rose or carnation in his buttonhole. He might have been dubbed "a motif in white," for I particularly admired his thick snowy eyebrows and fervently wished that my father would get really old quickly so that his own rather heavy eyebrows might become as impressively bleached (ultimately this actually happened, but by that time eyebrows were no longer of absorbing interest).

In those days the tall and picturesque forms of my father's brother Ernest and G. Bernard Shaw might often have been noticed stalking together down the central aisle of the Crystal Palace. They were both music critics on London evening papers, and I suppose as adequately equipped to pass judgments upon an art, of the technicalities of which they knew next to nothing, as some of our present-day pundits.

E.B.B.

Few people of interest came to the house at the corner of Clapham Common where we lived until I was twelve, and it was not to be expected that they should, for Nonconformist South London in the 'nineties was no den of eminent lions. Our only distinguished visitor was indeed my own above-mentioned uncle, Ernest Belfort Bax, and curiously enough his head was satisfactorily leonine!

Tall, handsome, stooping considerably, and always dressed in loose shaggy clothes and huge bow-tie, he looked more like a renowned painter than a rather clumsy writer upon metaphysics and sociology. He had been very intimate with William Morris, and together they had produced a distressingly bad book entitled *Socialism, Its Growth and Outcome*. (One of its reviewers wrote, "Each of these authors must have consented to send this work to press solely for fear of offending the other.")

E.B.B. was a very absent-minded man, and I doubt if he could have told offhand how many children he had. It is related of him that, while striding up and down the street in his quarter-deck manner somewhere near his own house, he stumbled against a perambulator. Roused by the shock of collision his attention was attracted in a woolly sort of way to the occupant of the vehicle. "A very nice baby," murmured my uncle dreamily. "Whose is it?" "Your own, sir," replied the nursemaid.

On another occasion, arriving at our house, he confided to my father that his braces had burst on the way and that he had tied his trousers with a piece of string which he had happened to find in his pocket. "But they'll come down, Ernest! They'll come down!" cried my father, all perturbation. "Oh, no," returned my uncle, negligently, "and anyway, damn braces! bless relaxes! as Blake says." "Blake!" "Yes, Blake!" with a smack of the lips, "Ah, h'mm!"

In his youth, before contracting the virus of Hegel and later that of Karl Marx, he had studied music at Leipzig and still played the piano in a slapdash kind of style. I always made him play Beethoven to me whenever he came, and once wept with mortification at realizing that he was then a rather better performer than myself.

CULTURE IN THE SUBURBS

In 1896 my parents removed from the south of London to Hampstead, and a far more interesting social milieu. "Here," confided the wife of a famous bookseller to my mother soon after our arrival, "we are not fashionable, only literary and artistic!" And Art was certainly rampant on the northern heights at the end of the century.

There were literary clubs, book societies, annual exhibitions of paintings by Hampstead artists; there were the Joachim Quartet at the town hall (with the old man frequently apt to play just out of tune), the Kruse combination, a standing dish at the Conservatoire, and an occasional visit from the Bohemian Quartet, then at its best. (I can still see Oscar Nedbal turning right round to face the audience, while his sonorous viola announced the opening phrase of "Aus meinem Leben.") All these concerts were a rich educational experience for me, for though I had been to a few of the "Saturday Pops" at the St. James's Hall I had hitherto known very little of chamber music, classical or modern.

SWEATED LABOUR

For a short time I took piano and violin lessons from an Italian ex-bandmaster. Never have I met a more accomplished sudorist—if I may coin a word—than that man. He held the perspiration record for thirty years, after which I believe a well-known orchestral director lowered it by one and a half gills. It is a fact, of which I can still produce eye-witnesses, that when Signor Masi attacked energetic music at the piano on a hot day his head literally steamed to the ceiling. Ultimately he was struck by lightning—so much moisture acting, I suppose, as a conductor—though happily not with fatal results.

A GARDEN OF LONG AGO

It has always been a matter of deep regret to me that I was not brought up in the country, but failing that, Ivybank and its garden could be counted the next best thing. The long rambling house, standing back from the road behind a semic rcular drive bordered darkly by laurel and ivy, was not old, and yet had all the air of being so. It certainly seemed to belong to the country rather than to a London suburb, for the window of my small and distractingly untidy study looked out upon a density of trees and shrubs through which not a sign of a house could be seen, whilst the garden was big enough to permit the unconfined personality of each season of the year to make itself intimately left.

Below the terrace steps at the back of the house was a large lawn screened from westerly winds by a noble row of chestnut-trees, ponderous with lamplike blossoms in spring, and beyond these a second green whereon all the summers of our youth Clifford and I, our friends, with one or two gardeners and policemen, played cricket to the peril of the adjoining greenhouses. There was a third little-visited lawn near the Belsize Lane fence, and we even boasted a small apple orchard—a lovely riot of pink and white in the early days of May. Roses, hollyhocks, sunflowers, and sweet peas luxuriated in that heavy clay soil, and for me the whole place was an island pleasance peopled with all the phantoms of adolescent dream, and I recognize now that my long-vanished garden played a more important part in the world of my youth than I knew at the time.

That same claubery clay soil was in the end to work Ivybank's ruin and final demolition, for with the coming of the Hampstead Tube Railway in the first decade of the new century there occurred settlements in the foundations and outer walls of the house, ceilings collapsed in the night, and the place was becoming a public menace when my father sold it in 1911. Almost immediately my old home was pulled down and the estate developed in a mesh of new roads and a pox of, no doubt, desirable villa residences. I can never pass the site without a pang.

WESTMINSTER

My pristine attempt at composition was coincident (very fittingly my enemies might snarl) with an attack of sunstroke when I was twelve. A sonata of course, no less! I continued to pour forth sonatas for two years until my father came to the decision that something ought to be done about it and carried me off to Westminster to consult—Sir Frederick Bridge, of all people, as to whether in his opinion a serious musical career was within the bounds of possibility for me.

(It was rather like an interview with a Harley Street specialist. "Do you assure me, Sir Frederick, that my son has really this musical taint in his system?" "I fear that I cannot hide from you, sir, that such is indeed the case. That will be three guineas, thank you, and mind the step.")

This elderly worthy, subduing the boorishness habitual to him (was he not to be paid by my father for his professional services?) deigned to admit that I had a better sense of composition than himself had at my age, a verdict that greatly pleased and impressed my father; though to me—even at fourteen—it proved precisely nothing in my favour. All was well, we backed out from the presence; proceeded, I remember, to eat poached eggs at a neighbouring A.B.C.; and from that moment my future as a musician was taken for granted.

CECIL SHARP

In 1898 I became a student at the Hampstead Conservatoire (now the Embassy Theatre), Swiss Cottage, an institution ruled with considerable personal pomp by the afterwards celebrated Cecil Sharp. This pundit was soon to build up a great reputation for himself amongst those numerous nationalist musicians who then believed that a true English atmosphere could only be achieved by "solemn wassailing round the village pump" (as Ernest Newman put it). The truth is that Sharp often talked a great deal of nonsense.

Soon after I had entered the school I attended a lecture of his entitled "Folk-song and Art-song." In his peroration he went so far as to insist that the melodies of the great masters, Mozart, Beethoven, Schubert, and the rest were scarcely to be mentioned in the same breath with the ditties of rustic Somerset. So much for your fanatic. But that was the era of the sacred pentatonic scale and the hallowed minor seventh, and Corder once told me that, listening to five works of young native composers one after the other, he remarked that each without exception began with a figure in the latter mode. It is true that one English composer of genius successfully incorporated these native nuances into a style which from the first had been unmistakably personal, but I do not know that the influence of the cult was otherwise very happy. This folk-song phase was inevitably followed up by an enthusiasm for folk-dancing, and as to this infliction I, for one, would have been happy to cry: "Their nine men's morris is choked up with mud." A sympathetic Scot summed it all up very neatly in the remark, "You should make a point of trying every experience once, excepting incest and folk-dancing."

ACADEMIC ENTHUSIASM

At the Conservatoire I took piano, theory, and composition lessons with an amiable organist, Dr. Arthur Greenish, a man who at the end of his days could make the rather dreary boast that he had officiated in the organ loft at the same Hampstead church for sixty-five years—or some such astonishing period.

In one way he was quite remarkable, for he gloried in the expounding of the theory of music. Imparting the mysteries of strict counterpoint to listless singing students aroused in him a spiritual exaltation, and did he speak of the chord of the minor thirteenth his eyes would fill with holy light. Whilst under him I bought "Tristan" and the "Ring," and found to my surprise that my professor knew little or nothing of this music, peering in a puzzled and slightly suspicious fashion into the pages of those dangerous-looking vocal scores.

In the latter years of its existence Greenish was the ever urbane conductor of my father's cherished private choral society to which

I had acted as accompanist since my thirteenth year. It was a tedious task for me, but I learned something of choral technique therefrom, and also how profoundly unintelligent most singers, amateur or professional, can be.

Usually we studied long-outmoded British works from the back shelves of Messrs. Novello's store, all by composers who by virtue of their mildness might well have been described as "sheep in sheep's clothing."

These were some of them: Sterndale Bennett's "May Queen"; J. F. Barnett's "Paradise and the Peri" and "Ancient Mariner"; Hamish McCunn's "Lord Ullin's Daughter"; and even some long work (name unremembered) by Sir Henry Gadsby. My father could seldom be induced to stray from these innocent pastures, although Mendelssohn's "Lauda Sion" and "Walpurgis Night" were tackled, and once we essayed "Acis and Galatea."

Before Greenish's day the choir had been directed by John Post Attwater, a humble but most accomplished musician, and no bad composer. This little man was peppery and highly strung, and at times, very properly losing his temper with the singers, proved anything rather than urbane. He it was who persuaded my father that it was time that I should study my art with a severer application than I had hitherto brought to it, and suggested the Royal Academy of Music. In September 1900, having successfully passed the entrance examination, my serious training as a musician began.

R.A.M.

The interior of the old Royal Academy of Music in Tenterden Street, Oxford Street, was architecturally a rabbit-warren. Somewhere about 1850, I suppose, the three eighteenth-century houses which the institution comprised were departitioned, one conjectured with fearsome violence. Even dynamite could be hazarded. Wherefore else the need for those tortuous tunnellings, that labyrinthine intricacy of passages, the cul-de-sacs, and follies? The bewigged and decorous soul of the original designer must surely have writhed in its rococo heaven (or maybe hell) when the fell deed was done. It took the average new student about a month to get his or her bearings, and though everyone was very kind and helpful there were tribulations for the less intelligent. One singing student of sixteen is said to have been found in a huddled heap outside Room 27 (a sort of *ultima thule* of the Academy), drenched in tears, and wailing at the prospect of never seeing her mammy again. However, by dint of hard experience most of us learned to find our way about in the course of time.

Entering the R.A.M. in September 1900 on the same day as B. J. Dale, the present curator, I found amongst my fellow students Adam Carse, Stanley Marchant (now principal), Eric Coates, Montague Phillips, Harry Farjeon, Paul Corder, W. H. Reed, and York Bowen. We were one and all composition pupils of Frederick Corder. Later on Myra Hess and Irene Scharrer arrived, as very small and eternally giggling girls, to study with Tobias Matthay, who also enjoyed the thankless task of trying to make me practise the piano and take an interest in his highly scientific (and be it added, dry) system of pianoforte technique.

Matthay, a benevolent Svengali, achieved magical successes with quite stolid and musically unimaginative students (not that Myra Hess is either), but his methods were often something of a trial to the highly strung. I, for one, could never play anything approaching my best at my lessons with him. It nearly always happened that just as I would begin to forget my self-consciousness and to play something like freely, "Tobs" would bump my forearm from beneath and cry excitedly, "What's this? Key-bedding? *To* the sound and no further, remember! Again now! Don't think of yourself! Think of the music! Beethoven!!" (and he would assume an expression and attitude of sublimity). "Beethoven's messenger!!!" (in a thrilling voice). "That's *you*!" and he would poke a long forefinger hard into one's midriff. Another trick he had was to charge one off the piano-stool like a heavy-weight footballer, and play the passage quite unintelligibly himself.

SIR A. C. MACKENZIE

In my time our principal was Sir Alexander Campbell Mackenzie, a man with a notable gift of frenzy. (This rhyme has been most effectively used in a lampoon upon Scottish composers in general by—no, perhaps better not tell.) The students' orchestra, which he conducted on Tuesdays and Fridays, presented a surprisingly stolid front to his strident shouts and bawlings, even though his Edinburgh accent became keyed up to tones of excoriating menace, or though, as on one occasion, he hurled his baton back into the auditorium. Those boys and girls never looked either amused or alarmed; their attitude was indifferent as that of a herd of cattle in a thunderstorm. Mackenzie from the first regarded me as a thorn in the flesh, and when rehearsing one of my tentative and irritatingly difficult efforts was wont to fling down his stick and ejaculate my short name with the effect of an imprecation.

Long ago in the heroic era—another Scot, Learmont Drysdale, dared to oppose claymore to claymore, and when at rehearsal of a composition of Drysdale's the principal broke out into his tantrums, the reckless student shouted back, "Then don't do the damn thing!" and snatching his score from the desk fled from the Academy for ever.

Mackenzie invariably brought his silk hat with him into the concert hall at these rehearsals, and on reaching the rostrum would place it reverently, crown downwards, beneath the conductor's chair. In a ribald caricature of "A.C.M." conducting, our irrepressible cartoonist, Theodore Holland, substituted for the sacred hat a certain humble but necessary article of bedroom furniture—to Frederick Corder's particular delight.

In his more mellow moods Sir Alexander could call upon a pretty store of wit. The story goes that when Elgar first entered the Savile Club as a new member Mackenzie ran across him in the smoking-room, looking rather bewildered and embarrassed. Though there was little love lost between them, Mackenzie, prompted by a kindly thought to put the younger man more at his ease, proposed that they should lunch together. It was a somewhat constrained and uncomfortable meal, but things were beginning to go tolerably when the cheese course was reached. Here Elgar appealed, "You know the ropes of this place, Mackenzie. What cheese do you advise?" "I think I know your taste," was the other's instant reply. "Why not try a little port Salut d'Amour?"

It must be remembered to their honour that in their own day both Mackenzie and Corder were enthusiastic progressives. The former introduced many of the most up-to-date works of his much-admired friend Liszt into the R.A.M. programmes, whilst Corder, ever an arch-Wagnerian, was the earliest translator into English of the master's libretti.

But neither was able to appreciate much music written later than say the death of Tschaikowsky.

Corder certainly admitted to a weakness for "Till Eulenspiegel," but, apart from his almost over-generous championship of the works of his own pupils, I never heard him express approval of any other music of modernistic tendencies.

He could see nothing in Debussy. One of his pupils, entering the classroom for his lesson, found his old master seated at the piano frowning in puzzled absorption at the score of "L'Après-Midi d'un Faune." Becoming aware of the lad's presence, Corder rose with that familiar volcanic sigh of his, and exclaimed, almost tearfully: "I've tried, *honestly* I have, but I *cannot* understand it!"

We are all alike. In the vanity and arrogance of youth we boast that no new development in our art could ever perplex *us*, and sincerely believe it. But after about the thirty-fifth year myopia sets in, and we are apt to make ourselves as ridiculous in the opinions of the next generation as our fathers and grandfathers seemed to us. To me, for example, and to most of my contemporaries, atonalism appears to be a cul-de-sac, cluttered up with morbid growths emanating from the brains, rather than from the imagination, of a few decadent Central European Jews. It is true that this idiom is now nearly thirty years old, and has never yet found favour with any save the actual personal disciples of its prophet, but who shall say with any certainty that the thing is worthless?

R.A.M. WORTHIES

Amongst other Academy characters of that day was Miss Riedl, the lady superintendent, and mightily suspicious guardian of the manners and morals of the feminine side of the house. This lady, an elderly German, was the possessor of a voice with an edge capable, I should think, when whetted up to full diapason, of demolishing a six-foot-thick wall. (Hey! a Mrs. Grundy armed to the teeth for you, my bonnies!)

Rumour had it that her fiancé was killed in the Franco-Prussian war of 1870, and that she had been permanently embittered ever since, poor creature. But oh! that barbed voice! Ear-pads were to be recommended when she and the principal hunted together in full and furious cry.

Then, of course, there was Green, the apparently immortal general factotum, with his lugubrious moustache, lachrymose eyes, and irritating habit of addressing or alluding to students either by their Christian names, or as "Mr. B" or "Miss C." Do you recall his rolling walk, flat feet turned out at right angles to one another, like the walrus in *Alice*—a gait alleged to be infectious amongst the R.A.M. professors?

He was elderly in 1900, yet in 1930 he had scarcely aged by a day, though I fancy he is now dead.

YOUTH

I remained at the R.A.M. for five years, eluding the Oxford career planned for me by my parents, and was happy over that long span as never before or since. My senses were drunk with Wagner, my nerves a-twitch to the titillating perversities that Richard Strauss was obtruding for the first time into a fundamentally diatonic style, whilst my brain staggered at that man's complex audacities of counterpoint and infernal orchestral cleverness. Wagner had made music the language of passion, and now Richard the second was turning the art into neurosis become vocal. Apart from Tschaikowsky, German music was all we youngsters knew in those faraway days, for Debussy did not reach England until the spring of 1905, my last year as a student.

By the way, my "A Celtic Song Cycle," written in 1904, was produced at an Academy chamber concert soon after the French composer's work was becoming known. One of the critics wrote, "This young man should be sedulously kept at present from further study of Debussy"—of whom I had never even heard at the time of the writing of these songs.

Most of my earlier music was treated grudgingly or contemptuously by the Press, but even when quite young I steeled my sensitiveness to all careless criticism, not willing that my

> Mind, that very fiery particle,
> Should let itself be snuffed out by an article.

Meantime in every hour not devoted to music I read feverishly all the literature I could come upon, poetry and prose, British and Continental. Clifford once announced that "Arnold has read everything, though no one has ever seen him with a book in his hands." A picturesque exaggeration, of course, but, though I do not care to boast of a critical faculty, my soul certainly adventured greatly amongst masterpieces.

I was one day eating up *Epipsychidion* on the top of a bus bearing me to the West End when the conductor, who had already collected my fare, suddenly reappeared at my side. Said he, "I see'd yer readin' poetry just now." Then bending confidentially to my ear, "Now, I'm pretty 'ot on poetry meself! Pertickler partial to Dryden I am. Cor! that's the bloke as can write! Gran' stuff!"

I wonder how many other London bus conductors have spoken as rapturously of "Macflecknoe" and the rest.

Any man must have been signed for ill-fortune at his birth who is not to prove the decade between fifteen and twenty-five the most exciting and illuminative of his life—even though he top the century mark in the latter end.

An eminent Frenchman once stressed his opinion that after twenty-five no artist can do more than attempt to re-live in his work the experience learned before he reached that age.

In one respect I have been the luckiest of mortals. When I was young I was thankful for youth and could have shouted for joy in my consciousness of it—and indeed, in my music, I frequently did so. In my 'teens I decided that twenty-two was the golden number in the count of man's years. I longed to be twenty-two and to remain at that age for ever, and I am not sure even now that I was not right. None of us students at that time had much money, we consumed eightpenny lunches at A.B.C.'s and getting home at the end of the day was a weariness of the flesh. But, pouring out our jejune imitations of Tschaikowsky and Wagner, we dipped our pens in the fiery fountain of Helicon, in unshakable assurance that no such music had ever before blessed the earth. Our masters might dowse the flame with cold water, but the heartrending disillusion of the evening was banished at dawn by the morning wind of a still more godlike inspiration.

And the lovely, bewitching entanglement of sex! It was all about us. Its unseen meshes were electric in the air through which we moved. I don't suppose there was any student who did not love, sentimentalize over, or lust after someone else in the place, and the accidental contact with the knee or shoulder of the girl of one's own (or even of some other's) choice would set live fire jetting through one's whole body. This it is to be young and still virginal.

No more than the next lad did I escape, nor did I wish to do so.

I found her almost at once amongst the second violins in the orchestra, sitting next to the aged and peering Polish professor with the unpronounceable name. Instantly I was enslaved.. Every Tuesday and Friday rehearsal I would make, rather shamefacedly, for the same seat in the hall immediately below her and watch her every glance and movement. I never thought of speaking to her or seeking for an introduction. I was too shy for that. Enough for me that when she was there those drear autumn days would turn to spring, whilst her absence made black midwinter shroud my heart.

And then, sitting in my usual place in the hall a little before the end of term, I started, with furiously beating heart, for amazingly her eyes and mouth were smiling down at me over the bridge of her fiddle—requital for my weeks of silent but, I suppose, obvious adoration. So it began, and at home that evening my lonely bed-room faded out and I wandered dizzily on the floors of heaven.

O youth! youth! The urgency of the triplets running through Walter's trial-song was the habitual rhythm of my mood in those lost years. Absolutely anything was possible of life, nothing too good to be true! Round the corner of the street one might find Land East of the Sun and West of the Moon, or a hood embroidered of spring flowers might half-conceal the burning eyes of romance in the old blue bus that toiled from Waterloo to Camden Town on the weary way home to Hampstead.

The glass-doored classrooms of the prudent R.A.M. authorities' decree put a check upon dalliance, but could one not somehow find oneself (and another) in No. 27, so remote as to be almost inaccessible? Something was bound to happen there as the spring twilight softly darkened that already dim little room.

I loved when I was young
The girls in all the bars,
And coming home I hung
My hat upon the stars.

I wish I could pay tribute to the name of the author of this excellent masterpiece, but I have never known it. It is true I have never so much as kissed any member of the class in which, I suppose, barmaids are included, except an Irish peasant girl. And that is all wrong too, for in Ireland, where the courtesy of the humblest cottagers is as fine as that of the aristocrat, there is no such thing as class-distinction, if manners, not riches, are the criterion. But anyhow the above lines have the root of the matter in them. There is no doubt that we used the wheeling constellations as our hatracks.

By summer 1905 my few particular friends were all gone and so the best of academic life being clearly over for me I gave up the Macfarren Scholarship, which I had won in 1902, a term before its full course was run. A phase of life was finished.

Though, I believe, quick-brained, I had been rather slow to develop. I always had to labour hard to acquire a balanced technique (my apprenticeship was by no means done with in 1905), and on the whole I had made little mark as a student except as a famous sight-reader.

R.C.M.

In 1904 the Patrons' Fund was instituted under the aegis of Sir Edward (now Lord) Palmer. The laudable object of the promoters was the establishment of funds to enable young British composers to hear their works rehearsed. From amongst these a committee selected a number sufficient to make up a concert programme, and a performance was given in one of the great London halls.

In the same year I managed to win the Charles Lucas Medal at the R.A.M. (there was little competition!) with a set of symphonic variations, and early in the following spring I received one of Frederick Corder's usual quaintly mysterious postcards, "Send me your variations by return of post. I can tell you no more now, but something may come of it." That was all, and I had no idea of his intention. But not long afterwards a letter arrived from the Royal College charging me to present myself there on a certain day in May for the rehearsal of my work. So that was what "F.C." had been up to.

The day came round (that sort of day always does!) and with it the beginning of a blistering heat-wave.

Now, hitherto I had never been near the R.C.M., and I had no idea of its manners and customs, though I always had a vague notion that it was a more aristocratic and pompous place than our old Academy. Quite likely, baronets and others of high degree abounded there. How, I asked myself, should one be dressed in the presence of Sir Hubert Parry? After careful deliberation I decided to be on the safe side and to array myself in my seldom worn frock-coat and tall hat.

The heat was intense during my journey to Kensington Gore, and I arrived at the intimidating portals of the R.C.M. already perspiring not a little. Shyly entering the concert hall, I started back, appalled at finding the place crammed with students and visitors.

It appeared that I had come in the nick of time, for Sir Charles Stanford approached me at once, and said brusquely, "So here ye are, you're Bax, aren't you? Well now, ye can go up there and work your wicked will on the orchestra."

At these dreadful words my knees knocked together and I stammered out in a very small voice, "But I have never conducted in my life." "Never mind that," retorted the ruthless Stanford. "You've got to begin some time, my bhoy. Go on with ye." There was nothing for it but to obey.

Over-harrowing it would be to resuscitate in any detail the pity and terror of that scene. I would naturally conduct with my left hand, and I probably did so then. But I really don't know, and from these words the perspicacious reader will have foreseen that in all my life I have never consented to handle the baton again. The embarrassment, the horror I endured on that sweltering afternoon! The orchestra players, I must admit, were stoically long-suffering, and only once did a politely ironic voice query, "Excuse me, but are you beating in twos or threes?" After some forty-five minutes of mental and physical misery Stanford applied the closure, and I stumbled off the platform, not far from collapse. "Ye look warm, young man," observed "C.V.S.," and taking me aside chatted very amiably for some time, incidentally giving me no doubt excellent advice on the subject of conductor's technique. But I remember nothing of that discourse, nor would it have served me in after life, for as I have said, in that hour I made my firm resolve, "Never again!" To crown all I had donned the detested garb of bourgeois respectability to no purpose except to make myself almost as hot and uncomfortable as I have ever been in all my days. For Parry was not there. I met him a few times later on, always consistently jovial, hearty, and old-bufferish. He was (incredibly) present at some performance of that early song-cycle of mine—I forget where or when—and at the end of the concert he bore down upon me—with his rubicund face, white moustache, and bright blue eyes, suggesting an incarnation of the Union Jack—smote me lightly over the side of the head with his silk hat, and roared genially, "You should have the words of your songs printed in the programme, my lad." I heard later that he had expressed the opinion that "Young Bax's stuff sounds like a bevy of little devils!"

Reflecting upon the three precursors of Elgar and the modern English "School" (a misnomer—we are all individualists, and no such school exists), I conclude that Parry was too ingrainedly the conventional Englishman. He was educated at Eton (where those playing-fields still are); he proceeded to Oxford where he continued to participate in manly British sports; he settled down as a well-to-do Gloucestershire squire, and I should not be surprised to learn that he was even in the position to present livings to vicars. He read and set Milton and the safer and more demure Elizabethans, and in Edwin Evans's phrase in another connection, "became an admirable 'prop to the pyramids.'" I can see him dining hugely with his spiritual progenitor, Handel, or hunting with enormous view-halloos in the company of Trollope, but I cannot divine any possibility in him of the "chaos at heart which gives birth to a dancing star." Such conservatism as Parry's does not propagate works of searching imagination.

If Parry was too robustly English, Stanford was not Irish enough. An Irishman by birth he belonged to that class, abominated in Irish Ireland, the "West Briton." There are intimations in some of his work that he started not without a certain spark of authentic musical imagination, but quite early he went a-whoring after foreign gods, and that original flicker was smothered in the outer darkness of Brahms.

Mackenzie, who began life as a comparatively poor man, obliged to struggle upwards, first by fiddling in inferior Scottish bands, and later as a rank-and-file violinist in the orchestra at Sondershausen, probably was more musically gifted by nature than either of the others. But he had no literary taste and little general culture of any kind. There was often charm and freshness of fancy in his earlier works, such as "The Dream of Jubal," and "The Rose of Sharon," but on the other hand he could be guilty, at his worst, of a drabber dullness than even that of Parry. (One of his last cantatas was most unfortunately entitled "The Witch's Daughter"; after the first and only performance it was instantly rechristened "The Ditch's Water.") His talent was too narrow and intermittent to permit of his work enduring.

Parry, Stanford, Mackenzie—they were all three solid reputable citizens and ratepayers of the United Kingdom, model husbands and fathers without a doubt, respected members of the most irreproachably Conservative clubs, and in Yeats's phrase had "no strange friend." Of this I am sure.

So pure was their moral tone that they regarded sensuous beauty of orchestral sound as something not quite nice (here I am paraphrasing an actual dictum of Parry's).

But unhappily all this array of social and aesthetic virtue was not enough, and it was left to the cranky and contradictory Elgar to prove to the outside world that even the despised Englishman could be a musical genius.

ELGAR AT BIRCHWOOD, 1901

Coming down to breakfast at Ivybank one autumn morning in 1898, I found my father seated at table, his favourite *Standard* open between his small and beautiful hands and looking quite excited. "You should read this, my boy," he exclaimed before I could take my seat. "A new English composer has turned up and the paper says that he is something like a genius!"

He handed me the sheet, and I read a long and highly laudatory account of the first performance of "Caractacus."

This was my earliest introduction to the name of Elgar, for although he was already past forty and not unhonoured in his native Worcester, I do not think that his work was at all known to the public at large, or that much of it had yet been played in London.

Eagerly I procured the vocal scores of "Caractacus" and "King Olaf," and was soon one of the composer's most enslaved admirers. Two years later to this admiration was added reverence, for "The Dream of Gerontius" took utter possession of what religious sense I have.

For its summer holiday in 1901 the family went to Malvern. There, incidentally, my parents were warned by a medical charlatan, preposterously in charge of a local hydro, that my heart was in so advanced a state of disease that I could not live more than a few weeks. There was matter for consternation indeed, but it could not be left at that and a "second opinion" was sought, with the result that next day on the Malvern College ground I was banging a cricket ball to the boundary and running hard between the wickets for my century.

In Malvern lived an Academy friend of mine, one George Alder, a horn-player, a wag of no mean order, and well acquainted since boyhood with Elgar. I saw much of him during that month of August, and one day he perturbed and delighted me with the proposal that we should walk over to Birchwood, the woodland cottage where "Gerontius" had been scored and where the composer was still living, and pay him a visit. We set out on a sultry afternoon, our heads in a cloud of gnats which we tried to disperse by energetic smoking, and as we approached the unpretentious but charming cottage I almost regretted my temerity in coming. My tongue and throat were dry and my heart a-flutter with nervousness, which was part allayed and part aggravated when we were told by a maid that Mr. Elgar was at present out somewhere in the woods. But he would be back at tea-time or soon after, and meanwhile would we sit in the garden where the mistress would join us at once?

The composer's wife, a pleasant-looking fair-haired lady, with— it struck me—rather an anxious manner, welcomed us very kindly in her gentle, slightly hesitant voice. Almost at once she began to speak enthusiastically and a little extravagantly about her wonderful husband and his work.

She spoke of her Edward's early struggles for recognition and referred to the rudeness of well-known literary men to less-known musicians, relating how Elgar in his young days had set to music a lyric by that notorious tough, Andrew Lang, and thinking to do the courteous thing, had sent the poet a copy of the song as soon as it appeared in print. Lang's curt response consisted of one sentence, "I don't read my poems when set to music." Alder and I here made suitably horrified noises, and our hostess was continuing, "On the other hand Dr. Richard Garnett was quite charming about 'Where Corals Lie,'" when I became aware of footsteps behind me. "Oh, here he is!" cried Mrs. Elgar, and I rose and turned with suddenly thudding heart to be introduced to the great man. Hatless, dressed in rough tweeds and riding boots, his appearance was rather that of a retired army officer turned gentleman farmer than an eminent and almost morbidly highly strung artist. One almost expected him to sling a gun from his back and drop a brace of pheasants to the ground.

Refusing tea and sinking to a chair he lay back, his thin legs sprawling straight out before him, whilst he filled and lit a huge briar, his rather closely set eyes meanwhile blinking absently at us. He was not a big man, but such was the dominance of his personality that I always had the impression that he was twice as large as life. That afternoon he was very pleasant and even communicative in his rumbling voice, yet there was ever a faint sense of detachment, a hint—very slight—of hauteur and reserve. He was still sore over the "Gerontius" fiasco at Birmingham in the previous autumn, and enlarged interestingly upon the subject. "The fact is," he said, "neither the choir nor Richter knew the score." "But I thought the critics said . . ." I started to interpose. "Critics!" snapped the composer with ferocity. "My dear boy, what do the critics know about anything?"

Now I have always been curious about other people's workaday methods, how long it takes them to get through a job and such-like matters, and so Elgar was asked what number of pages of full score represented his weekly average whilst he was working on "Gerontius." "Oh! about forty, I suppose," he replied carelessly.

Having at the time no experience whatever of the Egyptian labour that is orchestration, this quantum seemed to me surprisingly small; but now, after all these weary years at the grindstone, I realize that he might have spoken more boastfully. Particularly if he meant that he completed his pages in all that scrupulous detail which so admirably characterized everything he wrote.

Knocking out his pipe, he suggested that we might like to have a glance at a huge kite that he had recently constructed. We duly appreciated the lines of this mighty toy, though as there was no wind its excellencies could not be practically demonstrated, and were then led into a small wood adjoining the garden where we found Elgar's little daughter sitting on a swing. "Showing rather more leg than I care about, young woman!" remarked her father crisply. Thus admonished, the child dutifully slipped to the ground and I paused to say a few words to her whilst the composer passed on with Alder. The latter told me as we were returning to Malvern that during my short absence Elgar had asked him what were my musical ambitions. On being told that I intended to devote myself to composition Elgar had made no comment beyond a grimly muttered, "God help him!"

As a personal contact that youthful experience of him proved for me the best of Elgar. A shy captious man, he suffered neither fools nor anyone else with consistent gladness. His manner to others was a matter of mood, as many found to their disconcerted embarrassment. The next occasion on which I was to meet him was at the solitary festival of the short-lived Musical League held in Liverpool in 1909. He was there, in high spirits and his most genial temper. To my pleasure and surprise he called out on seeing me, "I do not need to be introduced to Mr. Bax again." Later at dinner he startled me by shouting up the table, "Mr. Bax! was it you who told me the story of the two-and-ninepenny crab?" whatever that recondite-sounding jape may have been.

In the following year I was invited for the first time to send in a work for performance at a Queen's Hall Promenade Concert, and when I went to Sir Henry Wood for a preliminary run through he told me (to my intense pride) that it was none other than Elgar who had recommended him to take up my work. It seems that he never forgot my visit to Birchwood (I think his days there counted as the happiest in his tormented life, and he kept a special regard for anyone who had seen him in those surroundings).

In later years I had two or three notes from him—one of them after I had forwarded the score of a string quartet on which his name appeared as dedicatee. He wrote "that he liked the look of it," but never came to hear it. The plain truth is that (apart from Richard Strauss whom he strangely professed to admire) he was totally uninterested in, and probably ignorant of, the work of any of his contemporaries or juniors.

On the death of his wife he became cranky and embittered, lost his religious faith (which hàd engendered a masterpiece), composed no more, and adopted the irritating pose of being interested in any topic rather than music.

The last time I met him was on his birthday in 1933. That evening Toscanini had given an ever-memorable performance of the "Enigma" Variations, and Harriet Cohen and I, with one or two others, repaired to the Savoy Grill after the concert for supper. There we discovered Elgar, characteristically surrounded by actors, Norman Forbes and Allan Aynesworth amongst them. Harriet, of whom Elgar was really very fond, rushed up to him and began vivaciously and charmingly to congratulate him upon the anniversary and the evening's wonderful music. With—as I thought—rather ridiculous affectation and ungraciousness, the old composer turned to his actor-friends and, spreading out his hands in mock mystification, exclaimed, "What on earth *are* these people talking about?"

DRESDEN, 1906-7

Dresden was a pleasant enough town in the early years of the century. It was perhaps rather too much infested by finishing schools for Anglo-Saxon misses (despotically governed by tight-lipped and disapproving spinsters of only too certain age). But there were quite enough stolid native Saxons as well; indeed in the Königliche Stadt-Opernhaus there were always too many of them. In my first spring out there I battened expensively on the fleshpots of the agreeable Bellevue Hotel, and the Opera House being on the other side of the square I was to be seen there three or four times a week.

This was a feat requiring considerable physical fortitude, for the aroma of that place was an assailant never to be forgotten. In these days, were I to return to the same conditions, I should very soon be sunk without trace. "The Germans rarely if ever wash, but the Italian washes once a year whether he needs it or not!" and the truth of the first part of that dictum was assuredly proved in the Saxon capital in the year 1906! That period must have been the heyday of the famous Dresden opera. All its most brilliant stars, Wittich, Nast, Eva von der Oesten, Burrian, Plaschke, Scheidemantel were still in the zenith. The director of the orchestra was then Edward Schuch, to my mind the finest conductor on earth. He had a very individual style; the first beat of the bar indicated by a strong upward thrust of the baton—a method I have never seen adopted by anyone else, except his own Dresden understrappers. Schuch had a really amazing control of climax and could sustain tension throughout the whole course of a Wagner music-drama. Even in the hectic furnace of "Tristan" the most blinding flame was saved for the final delirium of the "Liebestod."

On another and unforgettable evening the first act of "Siegfried" was taken at such a headlong pace that I could scarcely believe my ears, and yet the rhythmic poise and control were like those of a dynamo. And the orchestra that served him was perhaps the most magnificent that I can remember to have heard in any country.

The first production of "Salome'" was in the year 1906, and the cerebral lasciviousness of this piece of glorified eighteen-ninetyism was the tattle of the town. Its actual première took place early in January before I arrived, and I must have come in for about the fifth performance.

Burrian created a quite horrifying Herod, slobbering with lust, and apparently almost decomposing before our disgusted but fascinated eyes, whilst Wittich sang gloriously, although being long past her first youth and of somewhat generous charms, she scarcely suggested the lithe and catlike Jewish dancing girl. I was told that at the final *probe* she attempted the Dance of the Seven Veils herself, and that Strauss, sitting in the stalls, was so appalled by the spectacle that he covered his eyes with his hands and subsequently tactfully suggested that the double role was too cruel a physical strain upon the singer. It was arranged that her place for the episode should be taken by a professional dancer, who shortly before her cue was smuggled crouching through the stage crowd to a position behind the cistern in which Jochanaan was incarcerated. From here she ran out to take Frau Wittich's place before the footlights, whilst the panting singer took cover in her stead. (The effect was a little bizarre, for it would seem that Salome's complicated sexual inhibitions had in a moment caused her to lose several stone in weight.)

I believe that this is the course usually adopted, though long ago the enchanting Danish singer, Signe von Rappe, told me that she was allowed to perform the dance herself.

"Salome"—that unequal work, containing echoes of bad Liszt, the altogether atrocious Jochanaan music, and the brain-spun Seven Veils Dance—still, in such episodes as the theological wrangle amongst the Jews, and the portrayal of Herod's hysteria and neurasthenia, represents the composer at his most astonishingly inventive. Good and bad alike, it all seemed stunningly novel at that time, and at every performance the packed and suffocated house was thrilled. (The English schoolgirls pursuing their studies in Dresden were not allowed to go.)

But not everything in the Dresden Opera House was a breath-taking excitement. Lord! what awful operas my youthful curiosity lured me to endure! Unlike the Latin, who aesthetically will stand no nonsense, the Englishman and the German readily submit to boredom, and in some perverse way the former at any rate persuades himself that he is acquiring merit by its means. "The audience at a Queen's Hall Symphony Concert," once remarked Rowan-Hamilton, "wears a look of gloomy intelligence, of furtive expectancy, as though it were assembled for the practice of some secret vice." On the contrary, it is a display of virtue in public that the Englishman is after. No longer a churchgoer, he salves his conscience by going instead to Bach, and seeks to do his duty by his God in undergoing four Brandenburg concertos in succession without an anaesthetic. And when the final pedal-point mercifully arrives he experiences the same smug self-complacency and sense of thankful deliverance that his fathers felt when the Scottish divine pronounced, "And now, my brethren, seventhly and lastly." To suffer boredom and the ordeal by art is for the Englishman a penitential exercise.

The German, I take it, finds in works of such amiable dullness as Kienzl's "Der Evangelimann" and Lortzing's "Undine" the comforting mirror of his own better nature, and whilst it dozes under the dope of fatuous sound, its fellow, the primitive savage within him, can the more unrestrainedly get to work in devising some new *Schrecklichkeit* for the undermining of civilization. There is no doubt that he enjoys musical tedium in a simpler and more naïve way than the English.

An opera which I anticipated would be as tiresome as those mentioned above, but which turned out to be far otherwise, was Anton Rubenstein's "The Demon" (after Lermontoff), a work which in some of its numbers is as freshly national as anything by the members of the "Invincible Band."

The Prince's "Tamara" aria is a really ravishing melody, one of the finest examples of Muscovite (Wardour Street) pseudo-orientalism in existence.

Symphony concerts also took place in the Opera House from time to time. The programmes were, as the aforementioned Rowan-Hamilton wrote in the local English paper, "apparently designed for the satisfaction of those dear old ladies and gentlemen who like their Beethoven and little comforts regular as the clock."

But there were occasional sallies beyond the ring-fence of classicism. One programme included the second and third movements of Mahler's Sixth Symphony, and on this occasion I was introduced for the first time to the work of this eccentric, long-winded, muddle-headed, and yet always interesting composer. The restless perversity of the very individual orchestration excited me tremendously. I marvelled at the strange juxtaposition of the driest Kapellmeisterlich formulas and heartwrung melodies and harmonies which might have been the outpouring of a Promethean grief. And those gawky scherzos, interminable ländlers, with knobs on (and indeed, spikes!). These works of the oddly laboriously minded Jew are still a matter for squabbling amongst amateurs of the art, and I doubt if they will ever be fully understood, or even whether the composer himself had any vision in continuity of what he was driving at.

The reception of the excerpts by the Dresden audience that evening was anything but favourable, and when the conductor returned to his desk to direct "Leonora No. III" the applause was deafening, particularly from the English flappers in the *dritte Rang*. (As to these doves, all music unassociated with words was apparently passed by the censor. Even the frenzied and libidinous excesses of the Paris "Venusberg," or the frankly pagan and erotic languors of "L'Après-Midi d'un Faune" were not expected to be culpable of quickening the flush of guilty excitement or delicious shame in the virgin cheek.)

Speaking of the last work I may mention that I was present at its first performance in Germany, a very curious experience. Even the great Schuch could make little of it, and actual catastrophe seemed imminent at any moment. It was the only time I ever heard the Dresden Orchestra falter, but then it was likewise almost the solitary occasion on which I heard them try to play any but German or Germanized music.

At these concerts I also first listened to a symphony of Bruckner. Beyond its "heavenly length" I can remember nothing of it except its conclusion. The finale was cast in the shape of a formidably dull fugue, and as it showed signs of approaching its peroration I thought to myself that seldom or never had I heard any orchestra pile up such a prodigious volume of sound. It was at this precise moment that an army corps of brass instruments, which must have been crouching furtively behind the percussion, arose in their might and weighed in over the top with a chorale, probably intended by the pious composer as an invocation to "Der alte Deutsche Gott." The crash of silence at the sudden cessation of this din was as shattering upon the ears as the blow of a sandbag.

SCHNORR STRASSE, 1907

The following January I travelled to Dresden again, this time accompanied by Paul Corder, a colleague of mine at the R.A.M., and on arrival we found two more British composers awaiting us. One was Roland Bocquet, the writer of many very skilful but clearly Strauss-derived lieder. Noticeably handsome, black-haired and moustached, blue-eyed, straight of nose, and with a peculiarly beautiful speaking voice, he had been settled in Dresden for some years and spoke German like a native. He took himself rather Byronically, and posed as a blasé cynic.

The other member of our quartet I had known already in England and Ireland, Archie Rowan-Hamilton, flaneur and dilettante, descendant of one of the Ulster instigators of the '98 rebellion, full of Irish faults and weaknesses, but generous also to a fault. True he was but an amateur composer, but he had a recondite literary sense, and could flaunt a *fin de siècle* epigram worthy of the masters of that period themselves.

First there were lodgings to be found for Paul and myself. Bocquet quickly procured me a decent couple of rooms in Schnorr Strasse near the Böhmischer Bahnhof. Herr and Frau Ehlers, my landlord and landlady, had never before encountered an Englishman and assumed for some reason best known to themselves that I was Russian. (But that is nothing! Three years later I was taken by a commercial traveller in a Russian train for a Persian(!), though I should have supposed that blue eyes, fresh complexion, and rather light-brown hair were hardly typical Iranian characteristics).

Paul was much less fortunate in his house-hunting, for he was cozened into hiring a large dark room in a dingy hotel in Lindenau Strasse, which he found himself sharing with a family of bugs that leered hopefully at him from the ceiling as he got into bed.

Lord! what a drift of words went down the wind in the weeks that followed! We held a continuous symposium of youth, for though I, already aged twenty-three, was the youngest, none of us was over thirty. Sometimes we started at breakfast in one or other of our four lodgings (or rather three—for we drew the line at the Lindenau Strasse), host and each guest providing a previously specified item of the meal. All day it would seem that our aim was to "tire the sun with talking and send him down the sky." In the evening we would usually foregather at a *bierstube*, and, in the intervals of calling upon Trude for bock after bock, would tamper with every subject under heaven. We launched embattled argosies upon unchartable seas of speculation; we mauled the reputations of all composers and poets, living and dead; we unseated the very gods from their cloudy thrones. I once asked Roland Bocquet if he believed in reincarnation. His vehement and rather astonishing reply was, "My God, no! I don't believe in any incarnation!"

Despite all this disputation each of us (except Rowan-Hamilton) contrived to get through a great deal of work. I was engaged upon a colossal symphony which would have occupied quite an hour in performance, were such a cloud-cuckoo dream to become an actuality. (Happily, it never has!) Paul, a fervid admirer of Adeline Genée, was penning a ballet called "The Dryad," also destined for an imaginary stage in some castle of Spain—whilst Bocquet was turning out at least a setting a day of modern German poetry. Only Archie, a born procrastinator, did nothing, declaring as his excuse that "he felt saurian, lethargic as some great river-beast stirring heavily at the word 'pumpkin'!"

Sometimes we would all dine at Tiedemann and Grahl's in Prager-Strasse, or at one of the other more expensive restaurants in the town, and Paul and I would be secretly shaken with mirth over the anxious gloom with which Roland and Archie would argue as to the fitness of this or that wine as an accompaniment to Frisches Hummer, or Kalbs-Kotelet, or whatever it might be. They would approach the subject with all the careworn solemnity of cabinet ministers discussing a grave international situation. Perhaps, at the end of a quarter of an hour, Rowan-Hamilton, who always paid for all the wine (and cigars), would allow himself to be overruled by Bocquet, and one would have imagined that the affair was at an end. Not so! After some minutes of preoccupied silence on his part Archie, with an almost agonized expression on his face, would interrupt the flow of our discourse with, "After all, I must confess, I cannot feel certain that we were wise to order that sparkling Scharzburger! Don't you think that something a trifle heavier——?" And it would all begin again.

BÖHMISCHER SCHWEIZ

At last on a snowy March day I fled the town with a tall, calm-eyed Scandinavian girl. ("You are a regular Frühlingskind, Arnold," said the intuitive Bocquet sympathetically, hearing that I was about to leave, though I had hinted nothing about my companion.) We had decided to make for the district absurdly nicknamed Bohemian Switzerland, and in reality part of Sudetenland of sinister fame.

It is nothing like Switzerland, or anything except itself. (But perhaps, I reflect as I write, this is a false statement. A supercilious acquaintance, to whom I once mentioned the locality, murmured languidly, "Ah, yes! Very pretty, no doubt. It rather reminds me of the Mappin Terraces at the Zoo.")

We took train to the Austrian frontier where we chartered an ancient and tumbledown yellow cab, the floor of the interior heaped with none too clean straw. It was drawn by a scraggy and pessimistic-looking horse, and the bearded driver was so heavily swathed in rugs that he looked like a Russian *isvostchik*.

Bucketing out of the station yard, the man on the box incessantly jerking out curses and moaning complaints of the cold, we rolled and creaked into the woods.

My companion said she felt that there ought to have been an angered parent, foaming at the mouth, and brandishing a horse-whip, in close pursuit.

We huddled together for warmth, stealing rather awed sidelong glances at the white-drifted rides of that vast and gloomily romantic Bohemian forest. It was getting towards dusk, and it seemed not impossible that trolls from her country and native kobolds lurked behind every tree, or that—seeing that we were on the verge of Slavonic earth—the Baba-Yaga herself might come blundering through the branches with her monstrous pestle and mortar. However, after bumping through ever deepening snow for some miles, we at last drew up at the warm and hospitable Rainwiese inn, where we reckoned on staying for two or three days.

Unforgettable days they proved to be, poignant—sweet in recollection to my dying hour. By day we wandered in the endless glistening forest, gazed up at the mighty Prebischthur, or were ferried by a silent one, who may have been Charon himself, upon an ice-green water mirror, its breathless surface reflecting the tall frozen cliffs of the canyon through which the scarcely flowing stream sluggishly crept. Later, with the intense silence of the snow-curtained pines beyond the dark blue of the window, we lay wakeful in one another's arms half the night. And then . . . and then, no more! I can never discover how it was that during that strange virginal honeymoon—despite the urgencies of youth and unfulfilled desire—I penetrated into a fastness of peace and contentment, to which in all these long years I have never since attained.

1907-8

During the next year or so my life in England took on a slightly pre-Raphaelite tinge, for I was a frequent guest at Kelmscott House in the Mall, Hammersmith, then the home of H. C. Marillier, the manager of the Morris establishment in Oxford Street, and author of books upon Rossetti and Beardsley. I was even invited to live there.

The old sequestered house by the riverside was Morris and Burne-Jones from cellar to attic. The flowered wall-papers were hung with engravings by pre-Raphaelite artists, curtains and carpets were in perfect keeping, and on the wall above the study door was plastered a square patch cut from the very first experimental paper that Morris had designed. At the back of the house, enclosed by a high wall of ancient red brick, there was an old-fashioned garden, wherein at the right time of the year hollyhocks flourished in haughty magnificence and profusion.

Harry Marillier's wife, Christabel, many years his junior and dainty as a Dresden-china shepherdess, not only chirped and piped suitable Elizabethan lyrics and most incongruous comic songs in broad cockney, but also indulged in a ribald humour which consorted strangely with her delicately pastoral appearance. At her wedding reception after the fifth or sixth time of being asked by roguish local bores, "How does it feel to be the mistress of Kelmscott House?" she complained in an aside to me, "I do think I might be allowed to be the *wife* of the house—one must try to be at least superficially respectable in Hammersmith, you know!"

By way of Kelmscott House I came to know the Mackails. Professor Mackail—one of the handsomest human beings I ever beheld—had married Burne-Jones's daughter, and the whole family, father, mother, and their three children, Angela, Denis, and Clare, looked for all the world as though they had stepped out of one of the dead master's paintings.

Lady Burne-Jones was still living at the time, a gentle and lovely old lady, so frail-looking that in her presence one felt constrained to tread softly and keep one's voice low, for it would seem that at any strong vibration she might dissolve into pure incorporeal spirit.

The elder daughter Angela (now Mrs. Thirkell, the industrious

purveyor of so many graceful and witty novels) was in her teens a
rather breath-taking young beauty, and I shall never forget her as
she stalked up and down the drawing-room at 6 Pembroke Villas,
dressed in a gown modelled by herself after her grandfather's picture
"Sidonia the Sorceress." A somewhat formidable young woman
in those days, with at whiles an acid wit, and an assumed contempt
for men, which may have been mainly defensive.

I accompanied the Marilliers one evening to the house of Laurence
and Clemence Housman, where we found the walls of every room
adorned, like Christmas decorations, with Women's Suffrage
slogans, a daunting sight; whilst the Cause was almost the only
topic of discussion so long as we stayed. Back at home in Hammersmith, Harry heaved an exhausted sigh, mixed himself a stiff whisky
and soda, and gasped out, "For God's sake, my dear man! Sit
down at the piano and play me something light and lecherous!"

Up at Branch Hill, Hampstead, there still survived Miss Alice
Bird, daughter of a Doctor Bird, who had been Leigh Hunt's
physician and had (oh! how excitingly!) actually known Keats.
This charming old lady's mind was a jewel casket of heaped up
memories from a remote past, for she had intimately known practically all the painters and poets of the 'sixties. She told particularly
interesting anecdotes of Swinburne's youth, and possessed a proof
copy of "Songs before Sunrise" with the poet's own manuscript
corrections and alterations. Admirers of Algernon Charles's
phenomenal skill in manipulating the English language may be
shocked to learn that in his extreme youth he was unable to pro-
nounce his own name, and referred to himself as "Hadgie" (a nick-
name which in the family circle did not fail to cling to him).

CELTIC

In one of his autobiographical books my brother has told how, a
crass schoolboy of fourteen marooned by the weather at Totland
Bay Hotel, and with nothing congenial to read, he looked into a
volume of Keats for the first time, and even whilst glancing through
"Lamia" discovered himself to be a poet.

In much the same way I came upon W. B. Yeats's "The Wanderings of Usheen" in 1902, and in a moment the Celt within me stood

revealed. Now, I ask myself seriously, what exactly do I mean by this rather rhetorical phrase? It is none too easy to explain, for the word "Celtic" has been probed time out of mind with no entirely satisfactory result. In a famous passage the Breton, Renan, declared that "The Celt has ever worn himself out in mistaking dreams for reality," but I believe that, on the contrary, the Celt knows more clearly than the men of most races the difference between the two, and deliberately chooses to follow the dream. There is certainly a tireless hunter of dreams in my own make-up. I love life. I am an appreciative inhabitant of this world (or was, before it was delivered over to totalitarian devilry), yet a part of me is not of it. Of the implications of my earlier music Clifford wrote in a poem, "Adolescent dreams of more than life can give," and when I read of the warrior poet who forsook his father Fionn and the Fianna at the call of a demon leman, and wandered for three hundred years amongst enchanted islands in the dove-grey western seas beyond the ultimate shores of Ireland in quest of a content that he never found, even in the white arms of an immortal, then my dream became localized and I knew that I too must follow Usheen and Niamh from Ireland into the sunset.

In Dublin some years later I got to know a rather cranky English student of the Celtic genius, really quite a good old chap, though his manners were certainly rough and ready. A chance remark caused him to break out into an odd tirade which, though he did not know it, served to crystallize for me some of my vague intuitions about the Celt and my own Irish *alter ego*, Dermot O'Byrne, as he came to be called.

I had been lunching and wining him fairly well at the Bailey, and perhaps that fact may have partly accounted for his petulant eloquence. It was a lovely day in May and when—to mark time whilst the waiter set coffee and liqueurs before us—I commented on it, I was surprised to note the light of battle in his eyes. "May!" he growled. "You young fellows here in Ireland can't feel the true ecstasy of spring and never could. It's impossible!"

This man was quite unmusical, had only known me in Dublin and as Dermot O'Byrne, and never associated me with England or with any other life than the one I was leading at the time. On my remonstrance it amused me to be assailed as a representative Celt.

"Quite impossible," he reiterated vehemently. "Why? Because May-day is Hellene, an affirmation of this life, and this country is too inherently romantic (nowadays he would have said "escapist") to take any sort of pleasure in things as they are—a healthy secret known only to those civilizations that have passed through the purging flood of the Renaissance.

"Pan and Apollo, if ever they wandered so far from the Hesperidean garden as this icy Ierne, were banished at once in a reek of blood and mist and fire, and Gaelic poets of the later springs, in their restlessness and uncertainty of the tenure of life and love, sang ever of the lure of far-away. Fairy maidens entice heroes to enchanted islands in the western sea; Brandon and many others set out in curraghs into the sunset to find the Country-of-the-Ever-Young; the peasant singer invites his beloved to fly with him to Alban or Spain, or even no further than over the next hill. But never does poet—noble or humble—extol Here-and-Now. Cathleen ní Hoolihan is for ever complaining that she could be happy if things were otherwise—if the King of Ireland's son were at home—if kites and ravens were munching the four bones of the yellow Sassenach—and in punishment the gods have denied her the reckless and laughing rapture of the first days of May. You will never look upon your hills outside a mood that is a little preoccupied with beauty gone on the wind—with Deirdre's white feet in long-dried dew—with the wild geese, that fled from Ireland generations ago or are to fly back hither out of some future sky. The present is always illusion for you, even when the lark spins over your heads. You will never know the 'burly joy' of which Meredith sang in the English May."

Here he was obliged to pause a moment for breath, and to gulp his coffee. I, being of tender conscience and suspecting a personal application to myself in that generalized rebuke, had put in rather warmly, "Well! perhaps there is something in what you say, but maybe it cannot be otherwise. You know your history, I suppose, and you will admit that discontent with the present has not necessarily always been the fault of Ireland!"

And my excited antagonist, spearing again to the attack, had cried, "My dear boy! I tell you it's an inherent Celtic quality—nothing whatever to do with the miserable social history of the last few centuries. I know you are all fond of declaring that the mists and

forlorn ghosts of the so-called Celtic glamour are a foreign super-
stition set afoot by Macpherson's spurious *Ossian*, and supported
by the other popular fable that Ireland and the Scottish highlands
are always wet. You insist that the natural hues of your primitive
literature are gay and radiant. I admit that, but they are the gaiety
and radiance of the visionary other worlds, Hy-Brazil, Magh Mell,
Tír-na-nÓg—not of Ireland. You boast yourselves that the
stories contained in the Book of Leinster date from pre-Danish
times, and yet you cannot deny that all those sagas that do not tell
magnificently of terror and tragedy are concerned with those
other-world yearnings of which I speak.

"No! you are all incurable romanticists and only the remote has
charm for you. There never could have been a romantic movement
in Ireland because you have never been anything else than romantic.
Why! did not your Michael Comyn foreshadow the whole of
European neo-romanticism in his 'Lay of Tír-na-nÓg' at a time
when Goethe and Wordsworth and Coleridge were mewling and
puking in their nurses' arms? Celtic Renaissance indeed! How can
there be a rebirth of an idea that has never died? The Anglo-Irish
literature of to-day is simply a reclothing of the Celtic soul in the
attire of London and Paris. You people sing precisely the same song
of visionary lands that was voiced in the sixth century, and you will
continue to do so in the twenty-sixth if America has not swallowed
your soul!"

I went to Ireland as a boy of nineteen in great spiritual excitement,
and once there my existence was at first so utterly unrelated to
material actualities that I find it difficult to remember it in any
clarity.

I do not think I saw the men and women passing me on the roads
as real figures of flesh and blood; I looked through them back to
their archetypes, and even Dublin itself seemed peopled by gods and
heroic shapes from the dim past.

But I spent most of my time in the west, always seeking out the
most remote places I could find on the map, lost corners of mountains, shores unvisited by any tourist and by few even of the Irish
themselves.

Islands held an especial allure for me. When I sailed to Aranmore in the lop-sided old *Duras*, its decks littered with animated and heaving sacks (in which live pigs were sewn up) it was soon after Synge's *Aran Islands* had been published, and Kilronan was still exactly as he described it, even to the terrifying lunatic on the quay whose appearance and behaviour so horrified him. In Donegal I crossed from Burtonport to Iniskeeragh, a tiny flat ledge of rock completely swept by the sea in winter storms, "a poor wee miserable island," as one of the inhabitants complained, and there I visited the national school and found some of the most beautiful and intelligent-looking children I have ever seen. I lunched with a hard young priest, very down on holy wells and all other "superstitions," on the other Aranmore—off the Donegal coast—where nobody ever goes; I explored the holy island of St. Macdara in Connemara, and even Lettermullen and Gorumna, grim landscapes of stone where indigence and fever gauntly reigned. But for me all these faraway places were alike bathed in supernal light.

I spent many April weeks over a stretch of years at Renvyle House, at the south-western corner of lovely Killary, the ancestral home of the Blakes, one of the Twelve Tribes of Galway. The last remnants of this immemorial clan, finding themselves like so many ancient Irish families in much reduced circumstances, had years ago turned the place into a hotel—of sorts. And a bizarre enough hostelry it was! The house was very old, standing in a neglected demesne and surrounded by tall trees, raucously clamant all day with the voices of tumbling and volplaning rooks. Beneath the trees was a glory of daffodils curtseying to the winds of spring, the only season of the year in which I ever visited Renvyle. Not only was the house far gone in age; it was also extremely ramshackle, infested by rats and by a most pathetic ghost. The queer story of the attempt made by Yeats to exorcize this pitiful little shade is told by Dr. Oliver Gogarty, in his enthralling book *As I Was Going Down Sackville Street*. Mrs. Blake dominated the scene, a turbulent old harridan, clearly still living in the early 'eighties, for it appeared that any later period was merely fantasmal to her mind. Seated autocratically at the head of the table, during the progress of almost every meal she would scorch and wither the memory of Parnell and all other Land Leaguers with the devouring flame of her tongue, quite naïvely (or maybe cynically) regardless of the possible political

bent of her audience. She feared neither man nor devil, as accounts
from other sources of her own exploits in those same wild 'eighties
proved, but she once confessed to me her unutterable dread of
thunderstorms (an idiosyncrasy which she shared with Lord
Roberts—and myself!). She spen much infuriated labour upon the
task of finding her spectacles, which were usually to be discovered
high upon the bridge of her own nose.

I hated her politics, but all the same there was something heroic
about her. The other surviving member of the family was her
daughter, almost as ramshackle as the house itself, and wont—
careless of hygiene—to take six or seven dogs to bed with her. She
might have been the prototype of one of the more eccentric characters in *The Experiences of an Irish R.M.*

One of the features of the strange old house on that sea-fretted
edge of Europe was the very remarkable library. To this room I
was one morning introduced, with a certain unexpected pomp, by
the excessively cunophil Miss B. Therein were bewildering
numbers of books, none of them of later date than the eighteenth
century and some harking back to the sixteenth. There were even
Spanish books and manuscripts of the earlier period, a time when
there was much commercial intercourse between Spain and the
west of Ireland (the "Spanish Gate" still stands near the harbour
in the town of Galway). I should like to have prowled about those
mysterious shelves for days, but I got the impression that I was only
allowed there for this one occasion, and by a kind of special indulgence at that.

I do not know when that formidable old lady died or into whose
hands the place passed, but I fancy that there must have been a
considerable interval between that time and the day when the estate
came into the possession of its late owner, Dr. Gogarty. (The
Republicans burnt it quite efficiently for him during the "cross-
ness.")

Long ago now I was told by someone, whose name I have forgotten, that when the Blakes were gone there was a great auction
in the house of the furniture and other effects. (There were many
outstanding debts to be cleared off, I should suppose.) Amongst
these effects the library was included, and my informant related
almost tearfully how peasants of the neighbourhood were to be seen

staggering off under loads of those priceless volumes, most of them in all likelihood destined to be torn to pieces and used to light fires, wrap up butter, and for other easily imagined rustic purposes.

I worked very hard at the Irish language and steeped myself in history and saga, folk-tale and fairy-lore.

"Arnold, you have a completely Gaelicized mind," said "Æ" once, to my pride and delight.

By degrees a second personality came to birth within me, that Dermot O'Byrne who later on was to turn author and find his books accepted by Dublin publishers.

Thereafter I led a double life, for when I landed at Dunleary or Rosslare I sloughed off the Englishman as a snake its skin in the spring; and my other existence as a musician—still much under foreign influence—as an ardent cricketer, even as a lover of women, became almost unreal. For now I was in love with Ireland and for the while needed no mortal mistress.

Once free of the R.A.M. I spent more and more time alone in places lorded by the Atlantic and the dream-light of old tradition. As burningly as any half-starved peasant poet of seventeenth- or eighteenth-century Munster I adored my beloved in all her symbolic presentments—as Éire, Foghla, Banba—as Cathleen ní Hoolihan, Silk o' the Kine, or the Dark Rosaleen. In imagination I fought in her wars of old and dreamt cloudily of new and less material conflicts, of the long-foretold "Battle of the Black Pig"—to be fought out perhaps in the fields of art and intellect—that final victorious contest which should restore Ireland to her leadership of Western spirituality.

Oh! it was all, no doubt, very young and extravagant, but at times I know the mood and those dreams even now.

Under this domination my musical style became strengthened and purged of many alien elements. In part at least I rid myself of the sway of Wagner and Strauss and began to write Irishly, using figures and melodies of a definitely Celtic curve, an idiom which in the end was so much second nature to me that many works of mine have been called Irish or Celtic when I supposed them to be purely personal to the British composer, Arnold Bax.

At the same time I should like to put it on record that only once in my career as a composer have I made use of an actual folk-song. It never seemed worth while to write Carlow or Cavan rhapsodies.

I also dabbled in verse-writing from the first, though whether my many-coloured fancies had any literary value I had no idea. But these experiments were always an intense excitement to me, and the very slight manual toil needed for a finished result seemed a heartening miracle after the dreadful labour of getting a full orchestral score down on paper.

And all this I owed in the first place to Yeats, for his was the key that opened the gate of the Celtic wonderland to my wide-eyed youth, and his the finger that pointed to the magic mountain whence I was to dig all that may be of value in my own art. Neither does my debt to that great man end there, for his poetry has always meant more to me than all the music of the centuries, and at his death it was as though "The Hawk's Well" (of his own vision), which once in a hundred years plashed up the waters of eternal youth, had dried up for evermore.

All the days of my life I bless his name.

"GLEN"

When I was young there were two ways of getting to Glencolumcille. One was from the railhead at Killybegs, a decayed little port, pretty enough in rather a shabby style and particularly so early on a fine morning, with the sun low down above the Sligo hills on the other side of Donegal Bay. Thence it took you a mere matter of three hours on an outside car to cover those seventeen Irish miles to Glen, and during most of the journey on that rough switchback road you could admire the somewhat sinister Slieve League, one of the highest sea-cliffs in the world. Or you might go from Glenties, the terminus of the other branch of the Donegal light railway, from there you had twenty-three miles and four and a half hours' drive before you, and since even in winter I always chose that route (liking old O'Donnell the innkeeper, and the affectionate half-witted boots at the Glenties Hotel, and enjoying an awed glimpse of the firebrand parish priest and one-time jailbird, Father McFadden of Land League notoriety) I got to know something about the rigours of that north-western climate. There was no cover whatever on the now almost extinct "jaunting-car," and sometimes I found myself on a puddled seat even before I reached Ardara, to face Glengesh (a pass scheduled by the R.A.C. as impassable for motors) and the savagery beyond. Just after the Great War there was a short period during which, once you were in Glencolumcille, it was almost an accident if you ever got out again, for the horse-drawn car had become a museum-piece and there was only one motor in the place, about four miles up the mountain.

Nowadays a small motor-bus runs from Killybegs, carrying the mail-bags which almost fill the interior, and allowing comfortable room for two passengers only, although sometimes five or six are somehow crammed into it. (I have known what it is to be the seventh.)

But if you have been familiar with the place all your adult life you can travel there if you will in the wink of an eye on the wings of memory, and if I choose to go that way to-night from Morar, south-west through time over islands and sea, I shall have the advantage of finding ghosts awaiting me in Glencolumcille— humble phantoms of simple folk whom my youth held dear.

I shall find Paddy John McNelis the publican, seated outside his own door upon a pile of empties, labelled "John Egan, wine and spirit merchant, Sligo," his handsome patriarchal face with its full grey beard turned as ever towards the sea. No doubt that benevolent old shade will still be groaning one moment with the pain of his ulcerated foot, and in the next lilting some fragment of song in English or Irish. And what a reel of songs the old fellow had! When he was nearing his end and his memory beginning to fail I once found him, with tears streaming from his rheumy light blue eyes. "Och, it's a poor thing to be old," he lamented. "Sure there does be music all through my head, and it rising up to the roof of the house this minute, but I can't be minding it any more!"

And I know I shall hear the tapping of lame John Gillespie's phantom crutch from up the street, and in a moment he will be in the doorway, perhaps quoting Shakespeare at me, and then whilst his all too intelligent brown eyes wander bemusedly round the inn kitchen he will be complaining of the regulations at "thon house" (Letterkenny asylum, where he was an inmate for some years, and to which he returned to die).

D

I can still hear that poor crippled scarecrow, the rags almost dropping off his meagre form, asking me to send him a copy of Aristotle's *Nicomachaean Ethics*, whilst a cow stamped and mooed at one end of his dark and miserable cabin. (But lame John—or John Beg as he was also called—was a better scholar than the *seanachie* of old who introduced into his folk-tale a character named Harry Stottle!)

Then I shall step once again through the half-door of Cormac Molloy the weaver's cottage, just down the road towards the R.C. chapel, and hear the rhythmical rattle and shuffle of his loom, and—in a sudden pause—a greeting from the quiet pleasant voice of that little man with the girlish blue eyes and conspicuously well-washed face.

I shall see again the kerchiefed face of old Peggy, Paddy John's wife, her figure almost as round as she was high. I never forget how a coarsely jovial police constable, passing down the street just as Peggy was bent double in the act of sweeping up some rubbish, made a feint of measuring her enormous buttocks with his cane and guffawed, "Begorra! the biggest backside in Ireland!" to her spluttering indignation.

And there will be a stool for me at Sally Boyle's fireplace in the cabin at the back of the inn where I can admire her wrinkled old features under the white snood, and her general effect of a picture-postcard of the classical Irish *cailleach*.

I like to fancy that on my deathbed my last vision in this life will be the scene from my window on the upper floor at Glencolumcille, of the still, brooding, dove-grey mystery of the Atlantic at twilight; the last glow of sunset behind Glen Head in the north, with its ruined watch-tower built in 1812 at the time of the scare of a Napoleonic invasion; and east of it the calm slope of Scraig Beefan, its glittering many-coloured surface of rock, bracken, and heather, now one uniform purple glow.

In winter I would often linger at that window, too fascinated in watching the implacable fury of that same Atlantic in a south-westerly storm to sit down to work. At one end of the little Glen Bay was a wilderness of tumbled black rocks, for some reason named Romatia (a particularly "gentle"—or fairy-haunted place, I was told in Dooey opposite), and upon this grim escarpment the breakers thundered and crashed, flinging up, as from a volcano, towering clouds of dazzling foam which would be hurled inland by the gale to put out the fires in the cottage hearths of Beefan and Garbhros. The savagery of the sea was at times nearly incredible. I have seen a continuous volume of foam sucked, as in a funnel, up the whole six-hundred-foot face of Glen Head, whilst with the wind north-west a like marvel would be visible on the opposite cliff.

There were days when you had to lean hard up against the wind to keep your feet at all, and I have known stout Peggy to be actually bowled willy-nilly into the ditch at the side of the road. South-westerly gales filled my sitting-room with choking turf-smoke, and the only remedy was to ask the people in the kitchen to keep the back door open, whereupon there would be bangs and crashes all over the house.

Yet in that unearthly valley there always seemed to be a core of peace in the heart of the most ravening tempest.

The contours of Glencolumcille are themselves tranquil, very gradually falling for over three miles to the sea from "the Lachties," a rock bastion which completely shuts away the valley from the world to the east. Scattered through the glen are many curious upright stones, some of them incised with Celtic designs, and known as "crosses." They are indeed used on June 9th, St. Columcille's birthday, for the barefooted performance of the Stations of the Cross, but I have no doubt that they are prehistoric phallic emblems and figured originally in some dark sexual rite.

I am not a scientist, so do not know whether the fact that there is no land between the Donegal coast and the Polar ice has anything to do with the dramatic atmospheric and meteorological effects that one sometimes witnessed there.

One evening I saw over Glen Head the most astonishing and beautiful aurora borealis imaginable. Swords and spears of red and gold poured down the northern sky, with fanlike openings and closings of the heavens.

Another night in the midst of a furious north-westerly storm of wind and hail-showers Peg, who had for a moment been outside in the yard at the back of the kitchen, re-entered, remarking casually, "It would be worth your while to have a look at the rainbow," as though it was a perfectly commonplace thing.

That is the only time I ever had the luck to see a lunar rainbow, which is, I believe, a very rare phenomenon, possible only when the moon is full and the weather very wild. All the colours of the spectrum were there, although they were of course rather dim.

For some ten years I returned to "Glen," winter and summer, and came to know the people as I never knew any other community. "A hundred thousand welcomes before you," was their greeting on my arrival, and "Sure, we'll be lonely after you—thinking long we'll be," they would say when I left. All my winter evenings I spent in the inn kitchen playing "twenty-five" on the greasy table, perhaps with Paddy John and a couple of neighbours, whilst the house shook beneath the blundering buffets of the gale, each gust followed by a "God save me! that wind's a fright for ever!" from the womenfolk. Or maybe I would steer the talk round to the subject of ghosts and fairies.

At first the people almost always denied any belief in such things, but if I told a story of the supernatural myself I could rely upon its being capped by somebody, and at last everyone in the kitchen would be eager to contribute a personal experience or some hearsay evidence of the proven reality of the spirit world.

One night—it was dead calm for once—I was sitting as usual by the kitchen fire. It was very late, and none were left in the house but the McNelis family and myself. We were all getting drowsy and nobody had spoken for some time when there was a sudden terrific clamour at the front door. To my astonishment my companions all gasped, and staring at one another with naked fear in every eye, bolted to various hiding-places. One dived under the table, another lugged open the back door and fled into the night, a third shut herself into a cupboard. Old Peggy, trembling visibly all over, lit a candle with a shaking hand and went to open the belaboured door, so that I was left alone in the kitchen, wondering what on earth was up now. There was a mumbled colloquy outside and all at once an angry shout, followed by the sound of a heavy body lurching in the passage.

A stout elderly priest wallowed in the doorway, mad drunk. He peremptorily demanded more whisky from the woman of the house, blinking at me suspiciously the while.

"Who's the *fear dearg*?" (red man) he mumbled thickly. My

name was mentioned. "Bags!" he bawled offensively. "My name is Bax. B-A-X," I said with rising voice, for a wave of anger went over me.

"H'm," he grunted, seeming to lose interest, and then, gesticulating with thick arms, shouted, "Where are they all? Afraid of myself, is it? Hey! Charlie, Annie, come out of that!"

Whilst the pale-faced family unobtrusively reappeared, each one trying to find a seat in the shadows, Father X collapsed on to a chair close to me and engaged me in a deliriously stupid and, on his part, sometimes indecent conversation (there were moments when he obviously thought I was a woman). After about an hour of this he staggered out into the night.

Shaking with fury I shouted, "Who is that disgusting old swine?"

"Hush, hush!" said one of the men in horror. "He's a very nice man—a very nice man."

"What do you mean 'a nice man'?" I vociferated.

By degrees I found out the secret of all this odd behaviour. He was reputed throughout the three parishes of Glencolumcille, Carrick, and Kilcar to be a sorcerer, capable of appearing in two places at once, and of putting a blasting curse upon anyone who incurred his displeasure and especially denied him drink. I was told in a hushed whisper that not long before he had knocked at the back door of a public-house in Carrick after closing time and ordered whisky. The terrified woman of the house, realizing his condition, pleaded as excuse that it was so dark that she could not see a candle anywhere or find a matchbox. "Do you tell me that now!" roared Father X. "Next week ye'll not be fit to see anything!"

"And gorra," said my informant, "in a few days she went blind as a bat and never saw a stim, good nor bad, from that out. Now, boy!"

I heard that in his ordinary senses he was an excellent priest, a fine scholar, and a good musician.

Certain people in the glen were credited with the power of curing some particular disease, and I well remember a woman working in the inn being summoned from Garbhros to a child's sick-bed. I forget the nature of the illness, but the remedy was the recital of some Gaelic incantation, accompanied by breathing (or was it spitting?) three times in the sufferer's face.

The old custom of lighting bonfires on Midsummer Eve was still kept up, and, though it usually happened that the night was wet and misty, I eagerly took my part in the endeavour to make the Cashel fire the biggest blaze in all the glen. This traditional practice is, of course, pagan in origin, celebrating the glory of the midsummer sun, but like many of the elements of heathendom was easily converted to Christian usage.

The older generation took St. John's fire very seriously. I would see a few stacked-up turves alight in a potato patch and some beshawled old woman kneeling before it in prayer for a successful crop.

In old times sheep and cattle were driven amongst the flames, for the people had the idea that by a process of sympathetic magic the fecundity of the beasts would be increased.

Queer vagrants would appear in our valley from time to time. When I first knew it the place was cursed by droves of tinkers who would invade it, some forty at once, and settle down to continuous drinking and fighting amongst themselves for perhaps five or six weeks. They would quarter themselves upon the hospitable population and cause so much unrest and disturbance that the courageous and hot-tempered young curate-in-charge at last resolved to take the law into his own hands and banish them once and for all. Hearing that certain cottages in Garbhros were particularly infested by the "tramps," as they were called, he left the parochial house one night armed with a stout stick, and descending alone upon the townland strode into the first of the suspected cabins and, dragging the intruders from under beds and tables and from other hiding-places in which they had taken cover on the report of his approach, literally thrashed them out of the glen.

They never came again in such numbers or to stay for more than a day, but I once met a big crowd of them on the road between Glenties and Ardara, moving processionally, and headed by a man playing the fiddle and capering wildly to his own music. There were several gaily painted ass-carts lined with brilliant scarlet flannel, and containing some of the women and their grimy-faced brats. In one of them, alone and lounging languorously at her ease, was a red-headed woman, magnificently proportioned and gazing contemptuously about her with all the air of an oriental queen.

I think she belonged to the O'Rourke clan. Most of the Donegal tinkers were either O'Rourkes or O'Dohertys at that time.

There was one curious ruffian who was a frequent visitor. Mickey McConaill was reputed to be a wife-murderer; he was known to be often alternately dead-drunk and stone-sober three times in one day; and yet was in money matters a scrupulously honest man. If he went into a shop and its owner happened to be out on some short errand Mickey would take what he wanted, but always left payment behind him. He was remarkably clever at his craft, and in his rare bouts of sobriety played the violin very well and was deeply affected by his own music. I once asked him to play "The Coolin," but after a few bars he let his bow fall, and with tears running down his dirty cheeks sobbed out, "Aru, I can't play thon tune. It's too beautiful altogether!"

Another strange character was a diminutive lunatic tramp known as "Wee Kennedy." He would herald his approach down the street by a discordant din upon a mouth-organ which he called his "trump," and apparently imagined himself to be the Angel of the Judgment. Or he would cry out, "I am the wee *breitheamh* (judge). Let yez get on to your knees, the whole lot of yez, and make confession of your sins. Put up your *dean trócaire orainn* ('have mercy upon us') to God! *Tá an lá dearg na hÉireann ag teacht gan mhoill!* ('The red day of Ireland is coming soon')."

On one occasion he rushed into chapel during Mass and screamed out, pointing at the priest "Don't be listening to thon fella—he is Anti-Christ! It's the Black Mass he is saying, I'm telling yez! Let yez heed the wee *breitheamh* man!"

He was perfectly harmless, and quite happy if given a piece of raw fish to chew.

Rather to my astonishment—for such a thing must surely be unusual—I once heard a visiting priest tell the glen population from the altar-rails that they were the best people in Ireland, slightly qualifying his statement by adding, "If there are any better I have yet to meet them!"

That was the more or less superficial impression of a man who was almost a stranger, but I who knew those folk through and through continuously for ten years and intermittently ever since, can endorse that little-considered opinion with all my heart.

Those small dark-haired descendants of the aboriginal Iberian Celt treated me as one of themselves, and no greater compliment can be paid by a peasant community to one from far-away.

I shared almost every incident, whether at work or play, of that secluded world-old life between the mountain wilderness and the western seas. I took my part in digging turf and potatoes, I tried my unskilled arm and soon aching back at plying the sickle and reaping hook, I spent long golden September days (the most serene I ever knew) learning the detailed processes of the Donegal hay-harvest from "raking," "heaps," and "grass-cocks," to "tramp-cocks" and the final haystack. (This last was usually not finished until well on in November.)

Those people had their faults, of course. The women, quick of wit and humorously minded, might criticize one another's foibles unsparingly with words that cut and bit, though the very next day quite likely they would be doing their victim some good-neighbourly turn; whilst the men were carelessly cruel, like Roman Catholic peasants in other lands, to brute creation. But the good-mannered hospitality, and generous sympathy for the poor and unfortunate of men and women alike, might have taught a lesson to the aristocracies of the earth.

To the day of my death, and I hope afterwards, I shall continue to bless and love Glencolumcille and "the best people in Ireland."

THE MUSIC CLUB

In 1908 or thereabouts was founded the "Music Club," a dressy concert-cum-supper affair presided over by Alfred Kalisch, critic of the *Star*, and a pious thurifer before the altar of Richard Strauss. Kalisch was a lovable little man; in person—with his barrel-like trunk, thick colourless skin, squat features and habitual cigar, suggesting the gentleman constructed entirely of motor tyres who used at one time to figure in M. Michelin's advertisement.

The Club members were mostly elderly, and notable for wealth, paunchiness, and stertorous breathing. Bulging pinkish bosoms straining at expensive decollétages, redundant dewlaps, and mountainous backs were generously displayed by the ladies, whilst among the men ruddy double-chins, overflowing their collars at the back of the neck, and boiled eyes were rife. The assemblage indeed was ever inclined to bring to mind Beardsley's famous drawing—"The Wagnerites."

In the year 1909 Kalisch and the Club, seized with overweening ambition, decided to invite several eminent foreign composers as their guests, and to glut them with copious food, strong wines, and selections from their own works. The four musicians earmarked for these delights were Debussy, Vincent D'Indy, Sibelius, and Schönberg; and I may tell you at once that their sufferings were prodigious!

Though not officially connected with the Club—I was not even a member—it chanced that I played my modest part in all these outrages. My sight-reading facility was widely known, and it regularly happened that two days, or even but a day, before a Music Club evening, an envoy—it was usually Stanley Hawley—would call upon me, and snapping open a music-case, proceed feverishly to lay the catastrophic facts before me. These songs of to-morrow night's guest had been sent a week ago to such-and-such professional accompanist, and—would I believe it?—that inconsiderate swine had only just returned them with a note to the effect that he was sorry to inconvenience the Music Club, but it would be really impossible for him to get up the music in time. Hawley's eyes and voice would here become imploring and almost tearful. "Now we know that you can do it on your head, dear boy, if only you will. I know too it's a darned shame to ask you so late in the day, but we may—mayn't we—rely upon you not to let the Club down?"

Being young and a little vain of my one accomplishment as an executant, I never thought of refusing, though I was not offered a fee and was a trifle vexed that not once was it announced that I had undertaken a very responsible task at the eleventh hour.

As a matter of fact I enjoyed those evenings hugely, and derived much youthfully ruthless amusement from the social *gaffes* abounding and the unintended sufferings inflicted upon the unhappy victims from abroad.

Now Alfred Kalisch—or "K," as he was affectionately known to his friends—was as good-natured and well-meaning a little man as ever scribbled a press notice on the back of an envelope, but international tact was hardly his long suit. With an irony—tragic in the sinister glare of recent events—almost all German Jews have ever been loyal, and even obstinately loyal, to the *kultur* of the Fatherland. Music to them means German music; all the rest, if admitted to their attention at all, amounts to no more than the pretty prattle of intelligent foreign children. "K" was no exception to this generalization. I do not believe he cared for French music, for instance, or that he had any notion of the peculiarities of the Gallic mind. A few pots of beer or glasses of wine do not dope French sensibility to the point of amenability to almost anything as they might in Germany, but "K" could not realize this.

Of the four guests Debussy's torments were certainly the most excruciating.

The majority of the meetings of the Music Club were held in the Art Galleries in Suffolk Street, where the ordeal by two arts at once might be undergone by the more resolute British penitent, but for some reason that I have forgotten Debussy was led to human sacrifice on the boards of the Aeolian Hall. The proceedings were to be preluded by an address welcoming the composer, and embodying a short appreciation of his work. A speaker of French was an essential, for Debussy could understand scarcely a word of English.

Trouble began at once, for although Frederick Corder, who was a good French scholar, had been invited and had declared himself willing to make the address, he at the last moment failed to turn up, excusing himself on the plea of sudden sickness.

(The fact was, as we discovered next day, that his artistic conscience had worked mightily within him all the afternoon, and he had decided that he could not bring himself publicly to extol a musical idiom that he was unable to appreciate.)

His place was finally taken by Kalisch himself, whose French was of the school of Stratford-atte-Bow—or possibly of Oxford—it was difficult to hazard which, as he was largely inaudible.

The great composer, an inordinately shy man, was planted in a chair in the exact centre of the platform facing the audience. He was clearly utterly nonplussed, and could only attempt to solve his problem by rising and making a stiff little bow whenever he recognized his own name amid Kalisch's guttural mumblings.

This part of his ordeal over, he was permitted to shamble dazedly to the rear of the hall, where he confided to Edwin Evans that he would rather write a symphony to order than go through such an experience again.

I believe that a fairly representative programme of the master's songs and instrumental works was performed, and I remember that I played the piano part of "Ariettes Oubliées" for some American singer.

After the concert I had word that Debussy would like to meet me and thank me for my share in the evening's music. Never shall I forget the impression made upon me by that thick-set clumsy figure, the huge greenish, almost Moorish face beneath the dense thicket of black hair, and the obscure dreaming eyes that seemed to be peering through me at some object behind my back. As he lumbered vaguely forward, extending a cushioned hand, he looked like some Triton arisen from "the glaucous caverns of old Ocean." "A mythological survival!" I said to myself.

Recalling that morbidly sallow complexion of his I must conjecture that even so early the malignant foe, destined to be his death in his early fifties, was already prowling within his body.

Evans passed on to me the composer's remark that I had interpreted his songs very sensitively, but in rather too pianistic a fashion. This verdict interested me deeply, for never before had I been arraigned on the count of playing like a pianist. I wondered what Tobias Matthay would have said.

SCHOLA CANTORUM

If Debussy had undergone tortures of embarrassment, it was for Vincent d'Indy to endure austere agonies of apprehension, if I judged aright from the worried expression of his small, neat-featured, restrainedly hirsute, and inimitably French face.

Now d'Indy bore the reputation—perhaps unknown to Kalisch—of being one of the most bigoted and inveterate anti-Semites in France, and that evening's programme would seem to have been deliberately designed to exacerbate his foible. For the items—with one exception, small and quite unrepresentative solo chamber pieces and songs—were rendered one and all by the Children of Israel. But no! there were two participators of Gentile race—myself "at the piano," and my boyhood's acquaintance, Sir Frederick Bridge, the music-bacillus expert. Like most Frenchmen, d'Indy knew next to nothing of any tongue other than his own, and Bridge, who probably had never heard of our guest before this occasion, was unaccountably put up to make a few introductory remarks in English. Now to indulge in *facetiae* about a man who is not in a position to understand what is being said is surely to touch the nadir of bad manners; and that is exactly how the veteran of the Abbey organ-loft amused himself and his audience that evening.

The sole work of importance included in the programme was the then new Piano Sonata, which begins with that beautiful theme and variations, so resigned and mystical in atmospheric content, and played very finely and sensitively by the twenty-one-year-old Myra Hess.

Amusedly I noted d'Indy's expression of enhanced suspicion as she sat down at the piano, an apprehension made evident by the restless twitchings of his nervous face and hands. But after a few moments, his anxiety allayed, he relaxed and listened in calm appreciation, and at the end of the sonata expressed himself as delighted—albeit not a little astonished—that so young an artist could triumphantly overcome the complexities of such a work.

He endured the subsequent dinner with extreme politeness, and an air of long-suffering indulgence. I suppose there were more speeches and he must have replied, though of this I remember nothing.

Evans, a kind of liaison officer between musicians of all foreign nations and our own, presented me to him, introducing my name as one of our prominent composers. *"Mais il est si jeune!"* cried d'Indy with an accent of slightly contemptuous unbelief, but on my assuring him that I knew every scene of his fine romantic epic "Fervaal" backwards he thawed to a complacent smile.

Admirable was the gentlemanly urbanity of these two highly strung Frenchmen in face of fell adversities, and most instructive the civilized façade which they presented to our island crudities.

SIBELIUS (?)

Of all the human beings with whom in the course of my life I have become acquainted none, I should say, has altered more, during the last thirty years, than Sibelius. Physically he has changed much, but this apart, comparison of my impression of him in 1909 with that of 1936 might be of two totally different men.

The massive, bald-headed titan of the latter year, suggesting an embodiment of one of the primeval forces that pervade the "Kalevala," can at whim transform himself into a purveyor of farcical fun and Rabelaisian joviality. But the earlier Sibelius gave one the notion that he had never laughed in his life, and never could. That strong taut frame, those cold steel-blue eyes, and hard-lipped mouth, were those of a Viking raider, insensible to scruple, tenderness, or humour of any sort.

An arresting, formidable-looking fellow, born of dark rock and northern forest, yet somehow only half the size of the capricious old Colossus of to-day.

Such was his outward semblance, but can it be that on that evening of his London reception he was hag-ridden by an artistic conscience?

Now we do not know, and no one will ever dare ask him, what he himself thinks of that endless series of short instrumental pieces and songs which all his life he has poured out in opus numbers interlarded with those of such mighty monuments of an utterly individual mind as the Fourth Symphony, "Luonettar," and "Tapiola." With undeterred hope we continue to turn over these hundreds of pages, discovering nothing with the hallmark of the master upon them. These trifles are, with scarcely an exception, entirely undistinguished and characterless, nor do we find either improvement or deterioration as the years pass and the true Sibelius of the symphonies increases in stature and power. The elegy or valse written in 1930 might well have been dated 1890, and vice versa.

There is precisely nothing to them. They are not even bad, and never vulgar. The best of the songs are not superior to the average Tschaikowsky song, which indeed would seem to be their prototype. Has the composer some inexplicable regard for these banalities, and if not, why has he troubled to waste so much ink during his long career? These things cannot be pot-boilers, for when he was still scarcely past his youth the Finnish Government voted him a handsome life pension.

If ever this composer (already with the Second Symphony to his name) was troubled by artistic conscience, that London concert in 1909 must have caused him a more searching embarrassment than even that suffered by Debussy. Was that why he looked so grim?

As they had pledged themselves to an evening of Sibelius's smaller works, and since there was nothing better to be performed, the promoters of the concert were scarcely to blame, unless they may be charged with carelessly taking a chance with a growing reputation in that they did not first find out whether there was any chamber music of the composer's worth listening to. I believe that this lamentable affair was a serious setback to the acceptance in England of Sibelius's best work, and delayed the recognition of the grandeur of the later symphonies for several years.

And what of the old gentleman of Jarvenpäa nowadays? Since he no longer writes either masterpiece or rubbish can it not be that in happier circumstances his caprices would have become even more irresponsible as the years advanced, and his laughter still more Homeric? But, alas! there is nothing to laugh about in Finland to-day.

SCHÖNBERG

It was some four years later that Arnold Schönberg was entertained by the Club. I had the usual visit from Hawley and capitulated as before to his urgent and flattering entreaties.

In the Suffolk Street Galleries the same comfortable opulence was evidenced, and all was unchanged except that the tonnage of the audience was higher and its chins had multiplied.

It may be said that, compared with his predecessors, the Austrian composer was let down lightly.

True, the guest was once again regaled with a programme made up exclusively of his early works, but the philistine may urge that composer and audience alike were fortunate in having their eyes tickled by those innocuous post-Wagnerian sounds rather than assailed, as they might have been at that date, by the menacing vanguard of atonalism.

Schönberg, possibly to advertise his indifference to or contempt for the sentimentalities of his youth, kept the company waiting three-quarters of an hour, but when at last he was honourably seated in the front row and the evening's music was under way he looked quite pleased with himself. Not once did that bald head become roseate with the flush of shame or embarrassment; nor indeed was there any need, for all that neurotically emotional early work of his is extremely deftly written, even though it may be thought almost too flattering to Bayreuth.

Upon the later developments of Schönberg and his disciples I am not yet capable of passing final judgment, even a personal one, but I am pretty sure that atonalism as a means of expressing emotional states must be confined to those deriving from the diseases of the soul and body. As manifestations of neurosis in art such works as Schönberg's "Erwartung" and "Pierrot Lunaire," and Berg's "Wozzeck" and "Lulu" are unsurpassed even by the most liverish and kidney-racking scenes in "Salome" and "Elektra"; and I should think that the idiom might cope successfully with sexual inhibitions. But it is improbable that healthy and natural things like the coming of spring, young love, or any gay or happy idea can ever be associated with so turgid a medium.

RUSSIA, 1910

> Be warned by my lot, which I know you will not,
> And learn about women from me.

You will admit, readers, that hitherto this little book has been light-hearted enough. You have accompanied me upon easy paths in summer weather, and maybe you will have assumed that all my youth was blessed by uninterrupted sunshine. But now I bid you don your cloaks and hunt up your umbrellas and strongest boots, for heavy weather awaits us before the sun again breaks through.

I am to tell of tragic Russia, and a tragic young girl.

I first met Loubya Nicolyevna Korolenko at a friend's house at Swiss Cottage in the autumn of 1909. She was of Ukrainian birth, and of very cosmopolitan upbringing. Her father, Nicolai, was an ex-general of Cossacks and at one time had been one of the wealthiest landowners in the Poltava Government. Through some mischance or folly—I never was told the details—he later lost the greater share of his fortune, though managing to retain a precarious hold upon his land and the two houses that went with it. This estate was at a village a mile or two from the small town of Lubny, almost exactly equidistant from Kiev and Kharkov. Not long after the catastrophe, which coincided more or less with the revolution of 1905, the general became hopelessly insane, and his widow, a woman of violently Pan-Slavist opinions, having bestowed her husband in a private asylum in Kiev, embarked upon a wandering life in various European countries taking with her her younger daughter, Loubya. This step was indeed necessary, for Loubya, though little more than a child, had incurred a decree of banishment from Russia for alleged complicity in the democratic movement amongst the students of Kiev.

After five years of nomadic existence mother and daughter found themselves in Lausanne where Madame Korolenko became editress of a Russian quarterly founded for the promulgation of her political creed.

Loubya, now twenty-one and her own mistress, had tired of control and decided to escape to London alone. There she lodged at first with a semi-Italian family, glad of a paying guest, and later on in furnished rooms with the youngest Italian girl, Fiammetta, who was also weary of maternal authority.

Oh! Loubya was like a naiad for beauty—a golden Roussalka with ice-blue eyes! Lured by the fascination of her nationality and history how easily did I slip into absorbing love of her!—a disastrous and humiliating adventure, but one that I have never regretted, since it brought many an enlightening experience which I might otherwise have missed.

A simple though serious-minded young creature she seemed at first, eager for affection, and quite excitingly ready to respond to my desirous advances. Gifted with a natural flair for dissimulation and with the cold pure face, spun-gold hair, and graceful body of a water-nymph, there were times when she must have taken a perverse delight in playing up to the fairy-tale role for which her physical appearance fitted her. When in this mood she utterly deceived me, as indeed everyone else whom she met in London.

But it was not long before there were hints of darker things, though even then I was too bemused to awaken to stark fact.

Really that girl was sheer Dostoievsky; fantastically introspective, with the melancholy Slavonic distrust of herself and of everyone and everything about her. The confused mingling of destructive intellectualism that then was in the Russian air, the pessimism and occasional outbursts of suicidal mania amongst the students of Kiev, and the cynical frivolities of Vienna and Budapest had curdled her mind until she must have approached the borders of that madness which was her family inheritance.

She was ever ready with all kinds of histrionic tricks. There were hours when she would work upon my horrified compassion with veiled hints of danger through which she had passed in the revolution, with subtle suggestions of the loneliness ravaging an undeservingly misunderstood spirit, with calculated fosterings of moods of reckless despair, during which—staring before her and gnawing a corner of her handkerchief—she would threaten suicide or abandonment of body and soul to the most corrupt purlieus of the Russian theatre.

At the time, of course, I did not begin to realize that much of all this was playacting. I only knew that she was very unhappy, and that I loved her bewilderingly.

Emotionally I was floundering in very deep and turbid waters, and even to others signs of this were evident. My brother told me later that during those early months of 1910 the pupils of my eyes would sometimes dilate in broad daylight in a most uncanny way. I was not surprised to hear it.

Yes, I loved her—that tortured and enigmatic figment of beauty. She appealed to my imagination as a fair unfortunate heroine of some Slavonic fairy tale—a soul of gold, imprisoned in the gloomy tower of modern intellectualism.

Despite her chilly disbelief in all things under heaven, her vanity, which was like a cloak mercifully covering from her at times the self-contempt cankering her mind, was tickled by my simple worship of every excellence which—except her lovely little form—she did not possess.

I know now that she had not the slightest insight into my true nature. Secretly, I am sure, she despised my romanticism as boyish and sentimental, and mocked at my idealization of her ashen-coloured soul.

E

When she quite suddenly and inconsequently took the notion that her family required her instant return to Russia, the ever sympathetic Fiammetta wired me the news.

On receipt of this telegram (I was in Connemara at the time) I rushed back at once through a wild spring storm, and in the first five minutes of reunion with Loubya breathlessly asked if I might accompany her to her own land. She agreed to my proposal at once, flattered no doubt by so notable a tribute to her power, but wounded me bitterly a moment later with a plain hint of her surprise at finding in me such determination.

Any possibility of scandal would be quashed by the fact that Fiammetta was to accompany her as companion—Fiammetta, a girl with a prodigal capacity for selfless devotion to her friends, and treated by Loubya—according to her whim—with childish sulkiness, lavish affection and generosity, or deliberate cruelty. There would naturally be a good deal of talk at home, and I would be unable to bid good-bye to my parents, who were away in Italy. But, enthralled by my *belle dame sans merci*, I did not care. My father and mother would be troubled about me, but pain to someone seemed the inevitable outcome of one's simplest actions, and personal suffering was only then beginning to teach me a real sympathy with my fellow human beings. It has been said that any man under thirty who is not a socialist has no heart, and that anyone who is over thirty and still a socialist has no head. Abstract compassion for collective misery may come easily to the young, but the majority of people under thirty are well able to bear the sorrows of their immediate neighbours with equanimity.

And has not Nietzsche proclaimed, "Everything done in love takes place beyond good and evil"?

I met the two girls on the platform at Lausanne—or rather I avoided them there until the train started, as Loubya was surrounded by her family and friends, assembled to see her off. We journeyed to Berlin, where Loubya took offence with Fiammetta over some trifle and would not speak to her for hours. At last I, who had never yet been sent to Coventry, took it upon myself to remonstrate gently, and to my surprise and relief Loubya consented to make up the one-sided quarrel. From Berlin we lumbered over the weary illimitable Prussian plain, and at last reached Eydtkuhnen

—the German frontier town. At the next station we were—thrillingly to two of our party—in Russia! Truly the stately amenities of a Russian customs-house afforded an unlikely introduction to a reputedly semi-barbarous land.

In one corner was an ikon with a lamp burning before it; conspicuously displayed on the wall facing the door hung a lifesize portrait of Tsar Nicholas II; our baggage was politely—almost deprecatingly—examined by elegant young army officers in greyblue cloaks and with swords dangling from their hips. Every single object in our trunks was delicately lifted to the light, whilst sedulous search was made amongst books and magazines—not a page of the latter left unturned lest an unflattering caricature of the Tsar or an article derogatory to the imperial régime should be overlooked.

But the courtesy of everyone was overwhelming, and I am not certain that we were not even offered tea.

When, to my serious alarm, my passport was temporarily removed by a smirking official, Loubya told me that he was amused by the shortness of my name, and certainly when the document was returned to me I noticed that I had become "Baksi," in Russian script, a more seemly sound, I suppose, to the Slavonic ear.

We must have been two hours in that place, and it was midnight before we set out again by the broader-gauged Russian railway through dark leagues of birch and pine *en route* to St. Petersburg.

My earliest experience of that great and beautiful city was dramatic indeed, for we chanced to arrive on the evening of Easter Day. Bells thundered and jangled from every church with its cupolas and crosses awry; the Nevski Prospekt was a flooded river of cars and droshkys, pouring steadfastly westward towards St. Isak's Cathedral; every class of the people of the capital was abroad in the streets.

Before plunging into the swollen stream we consumed lemon tea and special Easter cakes—very sweet and sickly—in the hotel, whilst Loubya amazed Fiammetta and me by emptying jam into her tea and eating the resultant mess with a spoon.

On arriving at the door of St. Isak's we found the great church crowded to overflowing, in spite of the fact that a charge was made for admission.

("To-night only the rich can afford to pray to God," Loubya

overheard from a peasant in the crowd outside.) It was therefore decided that we should make for the Kazan Cathedral. Here, though entrance was free, the throng was less dense, but still the enormous building was too full for comfort, and in fear of being crushed or losing one another we dared not move far from the door.

Very confused and blurred is my memory of that utterly bewildering scene. The blaze of a thousand sacred candles, the gorgeous vestments of metropolitan and priests, the awed ecstasy on the faces of that superstitious Slavonic mob as those mysterious, complex and colourful rites were enacted. A dim phantasmagoria of sound and light—that is all that remains.

Back in the hotel at midnight Loubya cried seriously, "Christ is risen!" and kissed Fiammetta and myself soberly on both cheeks.

It was in Petersburg that the unhappy Loubya's true nature was first fully revealed. For a few days I lodged in the hotel in Litény Prospekt where the two girls were staying, but almost at once Loubya declared that she was known by many in the city and that there would be unwelcome tattle. Thereupon, willy-nilly, I was banished to the Hotel de France near the Red Square at the other end of Nevski.

Ruefully I drove off by droshky, my *isvostchik* (packed in so many rugs that he looked like a bale of sacking) turning round on the box every few yards with a rascally grin and raising a dirty hand with one more finger upthrust each time. "Two roubles!—three roubles—five—six!" The fare had climbed to ten before the hotel was reached. Here at my request the old ruffian was paid one rouble sixty kopeks by the concierge, and made off, no whit abashed.

Her object in getting rid of me was soon plain enough, for in a day or two the admiration-crazy child had entered upon a rather dubious affair (probably no more than extravagant flirtation) with an officer in her father's old regiment, an experienced social diplomat whom she passed off as an uncle, though later he turned out to have no connection whatever with the Korolenko family. Not content with this she also renewed by correspondence an old relationship with a fellow student of the Kiev days to whom she subsequently became betrothed.

By sending me to the other end of Nevski she showed me clearly that I was to make no more special claims upon her affection and companionship, at the same time clearing the ground for her volatile adventures.

As Fiammetta sorrowfully observed, "It seems as if she was making use of us in England, just allowing us to love her because there was no one else to give her admiration!"

Painful indeed was my own position, and before a fortnight had passed I was sorely tempted to return home. But this would have been hard on Fiammetta, lonely and harrassed as she was already; also, pride and a certain dogged fatalism, new to my nature, determined me to go through with the experience, cost what it might.

I knew that, in spite of everything, this novel and unpredictable world was going to be full of interest, and here moreover was fresh food for art, even though to the soul it tasted bitter.

Loubya kept Fiammetta very much at her beck and call, and many solitary days followed for me. To while away the hours Dermot O'Byrne came to the fore, and to avenge the chagrin of his fellowself wrote a tale of ancient Ireland, wherein the vanity of women met with a nemesis of peculiar savagery.

Loubya knew moments of compunction, and would occasionally visit me with Fiammetta, and once indeed she came alone to my room as dusk was falling and stayed until daybreak, giving all she had still to give. But it was an illusory comfortless night—I could not understand her motive, and somehow she seemed only half-real.

Although the dream that I had followed all those hundreds of miles had vanished before the hot breath of the Petersburg spring, I was still much in the company of the two girls.

In that month of April we sampled many and various features of Petersburg social life. We visited a gipsy cabaret, an enormous and gaudy place where we drank champagne until long after dawn (the stage performance was a disappointment to me after all I had heard of the wild brilliance of these shows). We saw and heard the famous Moscow Art Theatre Company in the "Cherry Orchard" at the Mariansky. We lunched at a Caucasian restaurant, where the waiters were attired in their tribal costumes with very ugly-looking daggers in their belts. Pallid chunks of cheese took the customary place of bread by the side of our plates. We drank a curious red Georgian wine.

One night towards the end of our stay we took train for about fifteen miles into the country to eat supper in a great park, similar to—and possibly identical with—a place providing the setting of a long episode in Dostoievski's "The Idiot." The light nights were already upon that northern scene with all their uncanny bewitchment, and I strayed down those trim *allées* in moody dream. The park was then the property of a rich young aristocrat and ardent amateur conductor, whose whimsy was to throw open his estate for the entertainment of the public solely in order to enjoy the delight of waving the baton before an audience, and that evening with the co-operation of an excellent small orchestra he discoursed extracts from "Eugen Onegin" from a bandstand in the centre of the grounds.

Finally we attended the last performance of the opera season. I saw "Prince Igor" for the first time, and also for the first time the Russian Imperial Ballet. By the latter I was so headily excited that I came near to casting myself from the dress circle into the stalls.

Before the opera began the curtain went up, revealing the whole cast in the blinding splendour of the array of ancient Scythia (according to Bakst—or was it Benois?). Led by Chaliapin, everyone in the house rose to join in the majestic Tsarist national anthem. (I was told that at an invitation gala performance in that same house —an occasion to be honoured by the presence of the Tsar—the management triumphantly succeeded in "papering" the stalls beneath the Royal Box with the initials "N.R." picked out in bald heads. Surely the kind of brutal buffoonery that Peter the Great would have delighted to play off upon his boyars!)

At the end of the month Loubya remembered the original purpose of her return to Russia and decided that it was time to rejoin her family in the south. We travelled by night to Moscow, reaching that fantastic city early in the morning, and left to myself, I spent the day seeing all I could of its exotic surprises. I passed from blinding sunshine to the cool grey-blue mist of the interior of one of the Kremlin's cathedrals, a sudden miracle of calm and mystical beauty; I admired the monstrous and renowned bell; I gazed in revolted fascination at the Church of St. Vladimir Blagény, outside the sacred gateway of the citadel—that wedding-cake in stone and gaudy tints—that architectural nightmare, and did not wonder that the aesthetically repelled Napoleon should have wanted to blow it up.

At teatime I rejoined Fiammetta and Loubya at the flat of one of the latter's friends. This must have been at about half-past four. At half-past five Loubya, who appeared to be enjoying herself for once, declared that it was almost too late to continue the journey to Kiev that day, but Fiammetta, greatly daring, pointed out that, as the train was not billed to start until eight and the railway station was in the next street, we might just do it. Unexpectedly Loubya agreed that there was a bare chance, and that since our sleepers were already booked, perhaps we had better make the attempt, and two hours later we sauntered round to the station.

(The Spaniard has little sense of time, the Irishman has less, and the Russian none at all. If you order supper at a first-class restaurant in Petersburg or Moscow you must not expect to be served within an hour and a half. Conditions may be different in these days—if there is any supper to order.)

Of Kiev with its majestic golden-domed monastery above the Dnieper we saw nothing, except the stalls of the sunflower-seed vendors just outside the station. We were now on the last stage of our long journey, and Loubya, almost gay in Moscow, sank into sudden dejection and scarcely spoke as hour after hour went by. Rousing herself at last with a heavy sigh, she said, "The next station is Lubny where we get out." We had arrived.

UKRAINE

Fair and smiling is the Ukrainian land, a fecund Slavonic Demeter. Its contours are not unlike those of the Chiltern Hills, but forests of silver birch take the place of the beechwoods of Buckinghamshire and everything is on a more lavish and prodigal scale. In that month of May a thousand cuckoos clamoured all day until I could have damned them to hell, and gorgeous rollers flashed from branch to sun-stained branch. The earth buzzed and drowsed with heat (even in late spring the day temperature averaged from 85 to 90 degrees) and it was so iron-hard that on any slope feet slid as though upon ice. By night the languors of the not very remote Orient invaded the gardens, woods, and hills. Never have I seen so velvety soft and deeply luminous a sky, wherein the stars seemed to hang, almost to hand, like ripe fruit, whilst all the dark hours the nightingales trilled and fluted their song of classic grief. But has not Gogol described the May nights of the Ukraine for all time in a famous passage in his *Evenings on a Farm at Dikanka* (a book widely plundered by Russian opera composers)?

As I have mentioned, there were two houses on the Korolenko estate, one a cosy, comparatively modern building where most of the household now lived, and the other a gaunt and neglected palace of wood with a shabby veranda along its entire front. It was used only as a bedroom annexe, and herein two vast apartments had been allotted to Fiammetta and myself. Thence after supper on our first evening (we did not meet the family until the following day) we were conducted by the general factotum Vassili, that absolutely indispensable man. Beautiful as a bearded angel, with small, delicate hands and feet, this Vassili proved to be the only responsibly minded person in the place. With faultless technique he seemed capable of performing every domestic task, and could cope with others more unusual into the bargain. For instance, every Thursday it was positively a matter of ritual for the gentlemen of the party to drive in to Lubny for lunch, whence they returned in the evening, conscientiously and elaborately drunk. Who but Vassili solicitously ducked the more incapable in the lake and spread them out on the bank to come to their senses? He was a craftsman too, and showed us a mandolin and a casket of wood beautifully inlaid with mother-of-pearl, perfect works of art, made by him in what spare time he had.

The old house was about two hundred yards distant from the other, and through the soft and intimate darkness Vassili led us towards it and the maniacal barking and snarling of half a dozen dogs. The two English strangers were certainly in need of that Russian Admirable Crichton at the moment, for as we were lightly informed next day we should have been in danger of being badly mauled by the wolfish brutes had it not been for the soothing influence of our guide.

In the morning we were introduced to the house-party. It was difficult at first to sort them out and some of them I may have forgotten. Our host and hostess were Lvof Kiriloff, a schoolmaster by calling, and his gentle and docile wife Olga, Loubya's elder sister. (No more complete contrast between two sisters could have been imagined.) Amongst the others there was a good-natured and well-informed colonel, very proud of his son, a singer in the Imperial Opera in Moscow. There was an elderly German lady who, as I noticed later, seemed to be for ever operating at the samovar. How she had drifted into this strange society and whether she fulfilled any other function than that of preparing tea I never discovered. And then there was Pavel Gregorovitch, a moth-eaten old fellow—said to be an ex-army officer, though no one would have guessed it. He had a passion for billiards, prepared for a *partie* at any hour of day or night; so often did I challenge him that I even learned to play the game in Russian—"red in the corner," "white in the middle pocket," and so on, all quite pat. (Russian billiards is confined to "potting," and a declared game. Flukes do not count.) Apart from the numerals this was about the only scrap of the language I acquired.

Finally—of those I recall—there was Madame Varvara—the wife of one of Loubya's Petersburg cavaliers—a cultured woman speaking perfect French, and quite tolerable, though sometimes amusing, English. "Monsieur Bax," she addressed me once at lunch in her sing-song Russian lilt, "will you have a little cold calf?" Highly emotional was Madame Varvara, and once after I had been playing parts of "Tristan" to her and one or two of the others, she enticed me into the garden and mooed at me sentimentally and almost tearfully. But I fear I was a disappointment to her that afternoon.

As an anodyne for my ache at heart I resolved that—once I could accustom myself to my strange surroundings—I would work with a fury of energy which should leave little time for brooding. But first, as there was no sort of piano in either house, it was necessary to hire one from somewhere—but how? Loubya happening to be in an accessible mood, I told her of my difficulty.

"Oh," she said airily, "that's easily arranged. Lvof Pavlovitch is going into Kiev to-night, and he will be glad to see about it for you." This seemed a satisfactory solution of the matter, but later in the day up came Loubya again. "Lvof Pavlovitch is rather anxious about that piano. He says he knows nothing about such things and thinks you had better go to Kiev with him, and see to it yourself." I groaned inwardly, but went.

After tossing sleepless through the night—in the luggage rack of our compartment, if my memory serves me—I rose dry of mouth and red-eyed to find my companion regarding me purposefully. Being a schoolmaster, he knew nothing of any modern language apart from his own, except a few halting words of German, but it was plain that he wanted to communicate something.

"*Können sie Latinisch verstehen?*" he managed at last. I shook my head. "*Sehr wenig.*" But he would not give up.

We were approaching the railway bridge spanning the mighty Dnieper, and in some sort of Latin, quite unintelligible to me, he began to tell me about the "*flumen.*" By the time he had finished we had arrived at Kiev, and alighting from the train went out past the sunflower-seed stalls into the streets of the city. Having kept silence for some five minutes (an abstention which always told hard upon him) Lvof Pavlovitch paused, pointing astonishingly to the door of a toy-shop. "*Herein,*" he cried in German. Well, there really were pianos in that unlikely place—two of them—one a deplorable relic of the lodging-house tin-kettle order, and the other a quite excellent Bechstein upright. The choice was obvious, and arrangements for the instrument's delivery at Lubny station concluded, we returned to the street. At once the good Lvof Pavlovitch became all perturbation.

After many futile attempts he contrived to make me understand that he had much to do in the town, and, fearful lest I might get lost, thought I had better return to Lubny as soon as possible. I was in no position to argue with him, though I should have liked to explore one of the oldest Russian cities, and to his unmistakable relief turned back to the station whence happily a train was about to start.

For the greater part of that torrid day I sat huddled in a sticky torpor from which I was roused with a jerk at each stopping place. On the platform of every village station the same stage crowd of moujiks was lined up—or so it seemed to me in my comatose state—and every man-*vanka* of them was exactly like Tolstoi!

Exhausted by the heat I reached the village at last, having spent fourteen out of fourteen and a half hours in the train in order to transact that tiny item of business. The Russian takes a pilgrimage like that as a matter of course. As ever, time is of no object, and such an expedition means no more to him than a bus ride from Hampstead to Oxford Circus would to us.

The piano arrived with startling promptitude, and immediately I sat down in my enormous room in that ramshackle old palace, eager to begin work. But the life about me was so odd and so foreign to all I had hitherto known that for a while concentration was difficult.

The dusty furniture, in spite of its subjection before I moved in to the walloping of quite an army of beaters armed with stout sticks, proved to be infested with fleas; the crescendo pingings of mosquitoes were continuous, and the loud and monotonous noise of the rattle used by the night watchman on the balcony to keep himself awake also served the same purpose in my own case; almost all day long the lovely birchwoods resounded uneasily to the hideous howling chants without which the women amongst the Ukrainian field labourers seem incapable of working, even in their own dilatory way. One would meet them every evening returning to their villages in barefoot droves, sickles over their shoulders, and still making that animal din.

One night I had an inexplicable adventure. There were several doors leading out of my room, and just as I had got undressed there was a sharp and mysterious rap upon one which I had never yet opened. Doing so now I found myself peering into a kind of enormous vault and the solemn peasant faces of some forty men and women. Their leader, an elderly man with shaggy hair halfcovering his eyes, and holding a candle high, began to speak earnestly. Shaking my head, and replying in English that I had no Russian and did not know what he was talking about, I closed the door and locked it. There was instant silence. Though I listened with straining ears I did not even hear them move away, and yet in the morning the place was empty. Those people no doubt concluded that I was deaf and dumb, for at that date the moujik believed that only one true language was spoken on this earth—Russian—and that the sounds made by foreigners were mere gibberish.

To this hour I have not a notion of the purpose of that strange nocturnal visitation, and next day my account of what had happened awakened no particular interest amongst the house-party. "Perhaps they were bandits," someone suggested, negligently. As far as I am aware, no inquiries were ever made.

To and from the modern house visitors came and went; grey-cloaked officers of tireless charm and insincerity; lawyers and students with melancholy eyes and haggard, restless hands—all kinds of people. Someone might write proposing a week-end visit, and stay for weeks. There also arrived in company of a young student—euphemistically styled his tutor—an imbecile brother of Loubya's, an amiable creature of pitiably bestial appearance, his almost utterly inhuman features seeming to mock his sister's beauty with a ghastly hint of resemblance. The student tutor, whose duties were depressing enough, turned out to be an interesting and affectionate youth and I saw a good deal of him, since he and his dreadful charge were housed like myself in the old palace. He would read extracts from *Crime and Punishment* aloud in French, straying up and down the veranda, and the impression he made was quite uncanny, for his appearance was the exact counterpart of my mental picture of the harrowed murderer in that book. It might have been Raskolnikoff himself, reciting his confession.

With added guests the management of the domestic life of the two houses became more and more haphazard and confused. Meals came at any time—two hours late often enough. The tender-hearted but woolly-minded Olga Kiriloff's attention was almost wholly occupied with a crèche of crippled peasant children whom she had generously adopted; Loubya was by nature anything but a housewife; and even Vassili could not be everywhere at once.

A careless disorder reigned supreme. Once when the house was in the throes of some particularly harum-scarum domestic muddle, Madame Varvara whispered anxiously in my ear, "Monsier Bax! I do hope you don't regard this ménage as a typical example of a Russian country house. Even we think it rather odd!"

As spring turned to summer Thursday was not the only day for noontide excursions to Lubny, where champagne seemed to flow like a torrent at almost every hour. And always there persisted an endless, endless babble of feverish talk. Talk! Talk! Let the tongue never cease wagging, lest you hear your heart's blood ticking out her tale of wasted time, lest the brain and spirit turn sick with the questions that ransack their wounds wherever silence falls!

Through it all I endured in a vast but, in the end, quite tranquil loneliness, accumulating impressions for future service to my art, and holding a firm control over my ever present pain.

I felt very detached from this alien life, detached now even from the imaginary Loubya of my early dream. Herself I seldom saw except at mealtimes, and if we did meet by chance at another hour her only greeting was usually a wooden resentful stare of her ice-blue eyes, but I think now that once and again her conscience was troubled about me, and this discomfort, with her usual perversity, she visited upon its innocent cause.

I stayed over her betrothal party, a protracted and—for a time—very ceremonious affair. Guests arrived from all over the country-side—amiable military gentlemen, and various young Natashas and Olgushkas, alert and twittering with curiosity and excitement.

The feasting began some three hours late, but Vassili, establishing a firm control, had worked a miracle of organization. According to plan most of the company, including the bride-to-be and myself—though not Fiammetta—became very drunk. (I had to drink that night to drown obtrusive and ironic memories.) Quite early Loubya was assisted to her room in an almost suicidal condition of misery and self-disgust.

I left a day or two later, Loubya and Fiammetta driving with me to Lubny station. We all three made an attempt to carry it off carelessly, but at the final parting there was a slight break in Loubya's voice as she murmured, "Oh, Arnold, I am afraid your visit to Russia has been nothing to you but an evil dream!"

"No, no, Loubya," I replied steadily. "It has all been very interesting." Then she kissed me softly, and that was the end. I never saw her again.

I returned to England bruised in spirit, but with a strong sense of relief, a strange satisfaction that one episode in my life had been rounded off, irrevocably finished. No soiled rags or withered and sick-smelling flowers remained littered about my heart to mock me. I was grateful for this experience, thankful even for the morti-fication it had involved. Soon the ache was quite dead, and remem-bered beauty but the last pallid ray of a wild star in the rising of a new dawn. I felt enlarged in my sympathies by the clarifying flame of that almost forgotten pain.

But after all that was not quite the end.

One day, almost exactly twenty years later, I received a letter with a stamp of the U.S.S.R. at the right-hand corner of the envelope. Curious! I thought, whom do I know in Russia? Looking more closely I was amazed to see that it was addressed to Ivybank, Haverstock Hill, Hampstead. How on earth had it reached me? For the old house had been pulled down the year after my return from Russia, and in the nineteen years since then I had had several different addresses.

Still here it was. There seemed something faintly familiar about the handwriting. Then my heart leapt and missed a beat. "My God!" I exclaimed under my breath. "Impossible!" Tearing open the envelope, I turned to the last page. . . . "My love to you, Arnold dear, from Loubya."

The letter was written in almost perfect English, though when I had known her the only word I ever heard her say was "Oll-rah-it!" (All right!) (We used to converse in execrable French.) How and where had she learned to write it so fluently and well?

In a daze I read the sheets through, rubbed my eyes, and began again at the beginning. This was not the Loubya of the bitter, heart-searing Ukrainian days. Here, instead, was an outpouring of simple and wistful affection, even at times touching on sentimentality. (Loubya sentimental!) She inquired with eager and gentle interest after my family and her one-time friends over here, and especially as to Fiammetta. Was she married and to whom? Did I ever see her now, and if so, would I ask her to write? (But when I delivered the message, Fiammetta, whom a harsh and ill-fated life had hardened, would have none of it, and coldly observed, "There would be no sense in beginning all that again.")

My thoughts rushed back to that long-dead past of which this letter was the enigmatical wraith. "A situation," I reflected, and wrote in my reply, "not unlike the beginning of a Turgeniev novel."

There was a succession of letters between us after that and I soon discovered the secret of her easy English. She still knew none herself, but in Lubny she possessed a near friend, Madame Vera I——, who was well versed in the language, and from Loubya's Russian sentences made a translation which Loubya copied out and forwarded to me. Ah, those letters!

Tender, patient, with all the crazy perversities of her youth purged away by the sufferings and privations she must have endured from 1916 onwards, she never complained of her poverty and ill health; indeed I only heard of her straits by degrees from Madame I——, who had soon after that first letter removed to Daugavpils in Latvia. From that time Loubya's notes were sent to her faraway friend to be translated, and I would receive the original together with the English version direct from that foreign town.

Vera I——, who must have been a most charming and devoted woman, would write to me also herself, enclosing Loubya's letters and telling me much about her tragic, but now resigned, and even courageous, little friend. The latter's husband had turned out a brute years before, and Loubya had perforce tried to earn a precarious living for herself and her daughter, Nata, on the stage in Kiev. (I reflected sadly that in spite of her early morbid inclination towards a theatrical career, so introverted a nature could scarcely foster any sort of talent for it.) I learned from Madame I——, as indeed from Loubya herself, that this daughter was her very heart's core, and that she was prepared to make any sacrifice for her passionately loved child. Altogether it was plain that Vera I—— looked upon her friend as little less than a saint.

Though they asked nothing from me I managed to send the struggling mother and daughter some trifling help by means of the Torgsin system, and Loubya's extravagant pleasure and gratitude were very touching. She even wrote that she had taught her Nata to bless my name.

On a morning of 1934 once again a letter with a Latvian stamp upon it lay on my table and opening it I found a short note and, for the first time, no enclosure.

"This is the very last letter I shall write to you, my friend," it began. My heart stood still, and for an instant I was unable to continue. But I guessed what was coming. Yes! Loubya was dead—of typhoid fever. Her tired body—weakened by undernourishment—could make no struggle against the disease.

Nothing was left of Loubya Korolenko but a strange and contradictory dream.

That was indeed the end.

PHILHARMONIC

"Well, I am convinced that advertisement is the secret, my dear
Arnold. We've all been too scrupulous, too much afraid of soiling
our hands. But we must stiffen up about this business of British
music—become harder, and I believe that advertisement should be
studied as an exact science."

"H'm," I mumble.

"It is by no means easy and certainly not intelligently understood
in this country! I don't mean, mind you, that we should go in for
that sort of thing!"

My theorist points upwards to the house-tops where a colossal
red "B" flames suddenly through the rainy darkness—like the
writing on the wall at Belshazzar's feast—followed, with a mech-
anical flick, by the rest of the letters comprising the name of a well-
known beverage. "Nor need we post up our portraits and the titles
of our principal works in meadows by the railway lines! No, advertisement—the science of advertisement—must be cultivated with the
utmost care and subtlety. Do you know, I have just been reading a
book—well, I am afraid, by an American psychologist——"

"Sounds bad," I grunt suspiciously.

"Yes, I know. But—well, it's extraordinary, I must say it interested me enormously. He goes most systematically into the whole
matter. It might have been written by a German."

I laugh shortly, and scoff, "Oh, you and your Germans, my dear
Balfour!"

"Well, you know, after all it's the old Deutschers that have the
method. Oh yes, they understand all that kind of thing—you can't
get away from it!"

Thus Balfour Gardiner, with whom I have been dining at
Pagani's before a Philharmonic Concert at Queen's Hall.

A new work of mine is in the programme, and it is with but
half my attention that I listen to my friend's discourse. As we turn
into Riding House Street my heart beats faster, and for one instant
a kind of panic seizes me and an absurd impulse to go home at
once. The light of a street lamp reveals the raindrops glistening on
the ends of my black evening-dress trousers and the sight of these
garments reminds me that I shall have to appear upon the platform

after my work has been played, a curious show for hundreds of pairs of indifferent or hostile eyes. Lately I have been beginning to realize that my music is often difficult to understand at a first hearing, even to experienced musicians, and the perfunctory applause at the close of a novelty always seems a little degrading, mocking the emotion which has given birth to the piece.

At the orchestra door the players are arriving, cursing at the weather, and chaffing one another with the obscure type of banter apparently peculiar to bandsmen. In spite of the poor light we are recognized as we make our way through the group. "Good luck to the work!" cries out someone. "It went pretty well at the end of the morning, didn't you think?" and I feel a somewhat exaggerated gratitude to the speaker.

The principal entrance is thronged with taxis and motor-broughams, and under the brightly lit portico red-faced men in evening dress and gibus hats and expensive and glittering dowagers are ascending the steps with that air of self-conscious and dignified complacence natural to the Britisher patronizing one of the more abstract and serious arts.

Clustering volubly in the vestibule or lurking in the dark corners amongst the hoardings around the entrance are bevies of students from the various colleges of music. Their chatter is so mercurial, and so electric are their movements, that they produce the illusion of diving in and out among the legs of the steady procession of elderly magnificence that the motors continuously pour forth. These youngsters make but little effort to check the abandon of manners usual in their school refreshment rooms, and every new arrival of their own kind is hailed with shrieks and colloquial sallies —whilst the girls, if sufficiently attractive, are greeted with pinches and proddings from their high-spirited admirers.

Also are to be remarked those aesthetic and foreign-looking young men, darkly efflorescent of hair, their pince-nez only serving to heighten their eyes' fine melancholy, a class that would seem to have been born and bred in concert halls and opera houses, for they are never to be seen anywhere else—except perhaps in the Café Royal. They carry, a little ostentatiously, miniature scores of the symphonies or overtures to be played, and there are but two varieties— the dapper and the grubby.

F

It is five minutes to the hour, and we pass quickly up the steps, Balfour's round blue eyes peering shortsightedly through their glasses, and my own glance roaming restlessly from corner to corner. I notice some of the newspaper men, with most of whom I am merely on terms of distantly nodding acquaintance.

Oh! there are those two pompous young asses, Troup and Hansard, elaborately slick and knowing youths, who have only lately strolled into their posts from the world of university dilettantism; for you must understand that education at Eton and Oxford is an unrivalled qualification for responsible criticism of any of the arts, and especially of music. Besides, has not Troup actually published (at his own expense) a slim volume of inscrutable verse?

These lads cloak their native ignorance of anything but the superficies of music in a blood-curdling jauntiness of style, and particularly nimble are the jibes spluttered like squibs from their pens when they write of a new British composition.

I congratulate myself that I have never spoken a word to either of them and make no attempt to evade the—as it seems to my overheated fancy—rather contemptuous glances that for an instant they direct down their noses towards me.[1] Somehow the assumed hostility of the pressmen stimulates me and I look defiantly round the packed vestibule. All these people are going to listen to my work. This thought rouses me like a challenge, for though I know well enough that to the great majority the last bar will come as a

---

[1] It is impossible for the creative artist to love indifferent or hostile critics with any real fervour and abandon. As I mentioned earlier, for years I received very little sympathy or encouragement from any of the Press, with the exception of Edwin Evans, always my sponsor through pre-war German thick and the Franco-Russian thin of "the silly 'twenties." In the days of my youth the average critic apparently considered it his privilege to indulge in crass personal rudeness and to say almost anything, however wounding, of his victim.

I remember my horror when as a very young man I came upon a statement by J. F. Runciman in the *Saturday Review* to the effect that "the knighthood of Charles Villiers Stanford had set the whole musical world laughing." And a one-time pressman on the *Observer* compared the present writer to "the club bore" after one of the first performances of "The Garden of Fand" (I really don't believe that this work is generally voted as tedious).

This kind of ink-slinging was nothing better than gratuitous bad manners, malice, and a will to hurt. Present-day music critics and journalists are very much more considerate and sympathetic, and I am happy to count several of them amongst my friends.

welcome relief, yet what do these matter if I can be sure of getting to the hearts and stirring the imagination of even but a few friends! And I feel too a certain satisfaction (that I really rather despise)—a naïve delight in the mere power, this evening to be mine, forcibly to impose my personality for a quarter of an hour or so upon willing and unwilling alike.

"Time is getting on, Arnold," says Balfour at my side. "We had better find our seats."

Thank heaven, I have made certain of a place at the end of a row, so that I may have an opportunity of escaping without causing disturbance if my heart begins to give me serious nervous trouble, as it sometimes does in a crowd.

I sit down in my corner seat and try to compose my mind. After all, I keep telling myself, this is an event of infinitesimal importance even to my own career, and for my comfort I think of the current cynicism to the effect that in England the reception given to a new work matters very little. The main necessity is to keep one's name before the public, and the length of a press notice rather than its quality is the talisman to a growing reputation.

Yet the confusion of noises in the hall goads my nerves uncontrollably. It is almost time for the concert to begin and the attractive din made by the orchestral players tuning and playing in their instruments stirs me with that old thrill that it ever wakes in the musician, as memories cry to the returned exile at the sight of the hills of his childhood. Out of the turmoil, I can pick up phrases from my own work, the first trumpet and the bass-clarinet practising difficult passages. Suddenly one of the double-basses knocks over a stand with a clatter that shocks through my head and sets every nerve quivering. And somebody leans over from behind and speaks in my ear, a sharp hard woman's voice, offering good wishes for the success of my piece. I mumble my thanks incoherently, with an inane smirk, not realizing who the speaker is until she is gone.

Lord! this is awful! Why on earth don't they start? Surely it must be long past the hour?

At this moment, amid a rattle of applause, the conductor steps on to the platform, a tiny black figure, very straight and dapper, seeming at the distance to move stiff-jointedly like a marionette. As he turns to the audience to bow his acknowledgments the white of his shirt-front gleams startlingly. Turning to the right I become aware of a small dryad face beneath a cloud of jet black hair, and a pair of bright eyes, brimmed with mischief, peering at me round the very manifest bosom of a director's lady. Good heavens! the girl I met at that picnic in the Dublin Mountains last spring. Yes, of course, she told me she was a piano student at the R.A.M. But it is strange to see this elfin child here, and for a moment I forget my surroundings, feel again the sea-wind on the Three Rock Mountain, hear the scrooge of the trams on O'Connell Bridge and the screech of the gulls over the turbid Liffey, and . . . and . . . The fatuous crash of the opening bars of the "Benvenuto Cellini" over-ture bangs me back into actuality, and for a few moments I try to concentrate upon the neuroticism, at once strident and flimsy, of Berlioz's music. But almost immediately my attention is wandering again. I steal another glance at the girl. She is in profile to me now, her brow slightly frowning and her eyes fixed seriously upon the orchestra. She is dressed in white, which accentuates her natural pallor, and looks tired and very delicate. But what a lovely little thing!

Heavens! the bluster of noise the orchestra is making, and all about nothing, with no particular bass to be heard! It is like the gambollings of some monstrous footless creature—a drunken walrus, perhaps.

Schumann's Piano Concerto comes second on the programme, but I am too preoccupied with my own work which is to follow to pay any close heed to the performance. My eyes roam around the half-circle of near and distant faces about me. Next to me sits a depressed-looking young man, belonging to that numerous class of persons (noticeable in any audience) who are in the habit of diligently reading and re-reading the names of the orchestral players, announcements of future concerts, and general advertise-ments printed in the back of the programme book, and continue to do so from one end of a concert to another. Why they come is an insoluble riddle, unless it is to be explained on my own hypothesis that English people actually enjoy boredom.

My glance passes on to a young lady eagerly scanning the stalls through her opera-glasses and whispering at intervals—social tattle, I expect—to a languid man with a fair military moustache who is condescendingly interested in his companion's flesh. Now and then the girl's pale blue evening dress slips off her shoulder, and she settles it by coquettishly wriggling her arm with a flush and a sidelong self-conscious glance at her admirer.

My eyes move on slowly. I remember that after a recent radical reform had been effected in the personnel of the orchestra, Norman O'Neill had remarked that all that was needed now was a new audience. I can make out very little intelligence of any kind in this ring of faces surrounding me. The majority wear the stamp of long-suffering apathy, and doggedly bear the cross of culture. There is a certain look of perplexity not strong enough to disturb their—on the whole—benevolent listlessness. It would seem that these people have never quite made up their minds as to whether they are conferring a species of favour upon art or whether they themselves derive some obscure benefit or chastening from it.

The concerto comes to an end at last with a brilliant display of technique by the soloist, followed by the usual indiscriminate applause with which an English audience approves all executants, perhaps considering their performance as in some vague way a branch of athletics and therefore worthily upholding a national tradition.

It is now the turn of the new symphonic poem. There is a pause, whilst the conductor mops his brow and neck, and the players find their parts. To my disenchantment I find that the eagerness of my anticipation has cooled, that I had reached the peak of excitement and interest at the morning's rehearsal. The hall seems to have become unbearably hot, and I feel suddenly conscious of the heavy atmosphere of bare flesh and perfumed clothes and gloves. The audience stifles me. The white shirt-fronts of the orchestral players swim a little through the harsh glare of the electric light. It is difficult to breathe and I wonder if I am going to faint. I feel my limbs twitching uncontrollably. It is really intolerable to have to sit still in stiff philistine clothes, with the points of one's collar pricking one's throat.

Yet how stupid to feel like this when my brain assures me once more of the utter unimportance and futility of all that is going on.

Out of the corner of my eye I notice that the black-haired student is leaning forward, her lips parted a little, the flush of enthusiasm that the foreign pianist's playing has caused still in her cheeks. I think she wants to make me look at her, to call upon me to notice her interest in my work. Turning my head I find that her eyes are trying to catch mine. This accomplished, she smiles gaily and gives a little wriggle of enthusiasm with the same suggestion of slight exaggeration which had perplexed me now and again during that memorable day in the Dublin Mountains. But, oh again, how beautiful she is! And the flame of beauty burning through me, stinging my overwrought nerves, makes the great mass of lights in the ceiling swing backwards and forwards alarmingly. I turn my eyes resolutely towards the orchestra. Better to think of nothing, to shut out all externals if I am to get through this. Above all, no feeling! Damn this heart of mine! It is pounding like a piston. One! two! three! four!—and then a horrible pause, as though it were gripped by a malignant hand. A relaxation, a moment of dizziness, and now on again faster still. No, don't look at the orchestra. All that black-and-white is restless and irritating, moreover it all swims together sickeningly when my heart misses a beat. I look down at my own clothes. The dark smooth surface (by the way, I have not noticed before how shiny it is getting!) at least keeps still.

The music begins, a low deep throbbing on 'cellos, basses, and harps. The piece is called "Christmas Eve on the Mountains," and in it I have tried to suggest the sharp light of frosty stars and an ecstasy of peace falling for one night of the year upon the troubled Irish hills, haunted by the inhuman *sidhe* and by clinging memories of the tragedy of eight hundred years.

When I had finished this work I had reflected bitterly that the measure of my success in capturing this mood (unknown out of Ireland) must be commensurate with the misunderstanding of the music by a London audience, for to express these subtleties I had groped after a new idiom, and the only passages likely to be acceptable at first hearing were those in which inspiration had flagged and I had been forced to fall back upon derivations from other music. I know there are such moments in "Christmas Eve," and that they will be seized upon by the critics as the only elements in the symphonic poem of which they can get any clear idea. The vague impression made upon them by the rest will no doubt be attributed, as usual, to obscurity and diffuseness on the part of the composer. I listen, with bent head, my heart throbbing out a ghastly percussive accompaniment. After a few moments this subsides. I breathe more easily, and for a short time enjoy utter happiness, bathed in the pensive ecstasy I have myself evoked. I know that in this part of the work at least I have not failed. The sound seems to invade the hall like a creature with an individual spiritual life of its own. Surely this must carry conviction, must break down the barrier between my own soul and the great collective soul of the audience. Out of the corner of my eye I see the young beauty still leaning forward, her small face cupped on her hand, eyes bright with excited attention, and the dark head nodding slightly to the rhythm of the music.

How marvellously the solo violin played that phrase! Surely! Surely! . . .

Yet I dare not look up. A sidelong glance shows me that my neighbour is anxiously turning over the pages of the programme for the tenth time in search of some advertisement he may have overlooked. And then for an instant something down there goes wrong. What is it? Ah! the cor anglais has entered a bar too soon. I start as though at an electric contact, and my eyes snap up. The player discovers his mistake before anything can have been noticeable except by the conductor and myself, and the even stream of the quiet music flows on. But for me the spell is broken. Why be a coward? What does it matter after all? I look searchingly round the audience. Everywhere I see for the most part a dull perplexity, a forbearing indulgence. Over there a stout red-faced man is yawning. I notice the girl in the precarious pale blue dress whisper something to her friend who shakes his head as though expressing a humorous hopelessness. On the other side of the circle two matrons are murmuring together industriously, and an old gentleman of military appearance uncrosses his legs and crosses them again, swiftly throwing himself back in his seat and stroking his white moustache hurriedly and with impatience. And of course there is coughing everywhere. In the stalls I detect Robinson (of the *Wire*) in animated conversation behind the back of his hand with one of the directors, a somnolent pachyderm. Near at hand I am aware of Stockton (of the *Daily Yell*) regarding me with a mildly injured expression, and observe Hansard a few seats away at the back scrawl something on the back of his programme and show it to another newspaper man at his side, who nods grimly with compressed lips. I feel utterly dejected. The music has lost all meaning for me. Heavens! Will it never end?

Then comes a confused period of panic haste, of rushing downstairs, of banging upon a locked door, giving my name and being admitted to the artists' room—of consciousness of agitated voices imploring me to hurry and of finding myself somehow on the platform, the stony faces of the first violins surrounding me disconcertingly. Then, in the midst of a deafening and foolish noise, of bowing stiffly to a sea of faces. Strangely aware of rigidly grinning, as though my jaws and cheeks are sticky, and feeling that my own hands and arms are clumsy objects tiresomely in my way. Noise! Lord! What a light and noise! A blinding din, and a glare that seems to beat crashing about my ears. I am recalled twice, and then the artists' room again; awareness of the red and good-humoured face of a director before my eyes and a hand, like a sponge moist with stale soap, limply grasping my own; also of a blustering and rather inebriate voice, shouting, as from a great distance, "Bravo, boy! A howling success! Splendid! Splendid!"

BRITISH MUSIC

The decade between 1904 and the beginning of the Great War saw an awakening of interest in and patronage of native music such as had never occurred before.

First came the Patrons' Fund, though this was originally devoted to the interests of promising students, and did not until much later concern itself with the work of maturer writers. In the following year (1905) the Society of British Composers came into being, and under the presidency of Frederick Corder sought to facilitate the publication of modern British works under conditions more benevolent to the composer than those usually to be expected in the managerial office of the hard-boiled commercial publisher. This society did some useful work, but sad mistakes were made, and many jejune pieces by composers later to come to the fore slipped into print instead of their rightful place, the wastepaper basket. An early trio of my own which I madly allowed to appear in the catalogue of the "S.B.C." has become the very bane of my life; for the firm of J. & W. Chester, which took over all the publications of the Society upon the latter's official demise, has ever been the principal musical link between ourselves and the Continent, and whenever application is made to them from abroad for an example of my work that early derivative and formless farrago is inevitably sent out, with the natural result that European interest in me is stillborn. I cannot blame Messrs. Chester & Co. (who do not pay rent in Great Marlborough Street for the good of their health), since this trio is the only extended work of mine in their list; but I wish the devil would fly away with the whole remaining stock of the damned thing, and give himself ptomaine poisoning by eating it!

ENTER SIR THOMAS

In the autumn of 1908 was witnessed the primal blooming of that shrinking violet, Sir Thomas Beecham, and his actual début was, I believe, at a recital (at which I was present) given at Queen's Hall by some forgotten lady violinist. He arrived on the musical scene from Italy, his trunks stuffed with the, as yet, unedited and often almost incoherent manuscripts of Frederick Delius, together with the scores of mysterious operas of his own, the pages of which nobody else has ever turned as far as I am aware. Beecham for a short time revealed himself as the Führer of native art, and a major offensive on behalf of British music was launched. It began with reconnaissance flights by Sir Thomas who distributed leaflets over a wide section of the London front. Bricks were dropped also, but there were no serious casualties, and the pilot returned in safety to his base.

The first shower of leaflets actually fell upon the drawing-room in our own house, for my mother organized a reception to Hampstead art fanciers in order that Beecham and W. H. Bell (later principal of the South African College of Music) might address them upon the subject of English music. That evening full dress was *de rigueur*, and I shall always remember the abrupt arrival of Ethel Smyth attired in tweeds, heavy boots, and a deerstalker hat, Swinging up the room between white shoulders and whiter shirt fronts, she shouted in a parade-ground voice, "There I join issue with you, Mr. Bell!" and then suddenly catching sight of Sir Hamo Thorneycroft in the audience, "Hallo, I haven't seen you for ages!" ("A formidable old warrior, you know, my dear fellow!" Beecham once remarked to me in later years.)

A series of concerts was inaugurated, one or two English works appearing in each programme, the then almost wholly unknown Delius in particular prominence, whilst several symphonic poems by Bell, who was very intimate with the new conductor, were given and even a mild and rather hesitant essay in Celticism of my own. The rehearsal of that little piece was a source of crushing humiliation to its raw young author, for no orchestral work of mine had been performed since my student days, and such was my innocence of all practical musicianly matters that I was unaware that professional copyists have no bowels of compassion and seldom trouble to correct their own careless mistakes. The parts only arriving on the day of the concert at Queen's Hall itself, there was no time whatever for me to go through them, with the result that the rehearsal was a welter of wrong notes, through which Beecham ploughed without comment and utterly unperturbed. With help from Bell, and by dint of hours of labour (unimaginable to anyone lucky enough not to be acquainted with this soul-destroying form of drudgery) I managed to get the thing right by the evening. But any other conductor than the nonchalant Beecham would have declined to take the chance after the chaos of the morning, and I do not know what impish perversity prompted him to leave the piece in the programme. After all it went tolerably well.

A curious experiment was tried out in Queen's Hall at one of those concerts when Holbrook's orchestral commentary on Herbert Trench's "Apollo and the Seaman" was introduced. A screen was rigged up immediately in front of the orchestra, and upon it as the music proceeded the text of the poem was projected by a magic lantern at the back of the hall. It was so contrived that the reflected stanzas synchronized with the sounds intended to illustrate them, a sort of precursor of the "talkies." The screen entirely hid the conductor and orchestra from the audience, a fact of which Beecham took full advantage, conducting in his shirt-sleeves and even at one point exclaiming in a stage whisper, "My God! I've the most colossal thirst! Let me see—ah yes! the third trumpet has nothing to do for pages. Just run out and get me a brandy and soda, will you, my dear fellow?"

At the supper following the concert, as I heard from Bell, Beecham and Herbert Trench sat at opposite ends of a long table. Towards the end of the meal speeches were made, one of them an encomium of the poet's fine and now unaccountably forgotten "Apollo and the Seaman," which on that evening the magic lantern had brought to the notice of everyone in the audience. As the speaker resumed his seat and the applause was subsiding Beecham called indolently up the table, "Do you know, Trench, I really think I must read your poem!"

His interest in native music—that of Delius of course excepted— did not long survive his first stroll through the *coulisses* of Covent Garden Opera House. During the Great War (and for the benefit of some charity, if I remember rightly) he was induced to direct an exclusively British programme—ill-balanced and of unwieldy length. When it was over and he was putting on his overcoat in the artists' room preparatory to leaving the hall, he was heard to murmur complacently, "Well, I think we have successfully paved the way this afternoon for another quarter of a century of German music!"

THE MUSICAL LEAGUE

In September 1909 the self-confident Musical League came to birth amid a great clamour of tuckets and tabors, and almost every English composer and outstanding executant made the pilgrimage to Liverpool for this loudly heralded event. Even Elgar and Delius were present and the latter must have been on the committee, for I heard afterwards that, taking no part in the drawing up of the programmes, he only came to life when the question of a festival banquet was discussed and that then his solitary contribution was a West Riding voice reiterating at regular intervals, "What ye want is a cawld colleetion!" (an expression which seemed to have some kind of fascination for him, for a few months later he invited me to supper in a flat he had rented in Hampstead, and his very first words on my arrival were, "Ah hope ye don't mind a cold collation").

This festival, if very enjoyable, brought no new masterpiece to light, and though it was arranged to convene a second gathering the following year in the Five Towns the scheme fell through and was never revived.

Instead, after a lapse of two years the princely generosity and selfless enthusiasm of Balfour Gardiner set on foot the most ambitious plan for the encouragement and dissemination of native work that had ever been devised. Three Queen's Hall orchestral concerts consisting entirely of English music were organized, and the New Symphony Orchestra and the London Choral Society engaged. By this time each one of us was a little older and our work nearer to maturity, and Balfour put together some really attractive and well arranged programmes.

In the following year he persevered and repeated the experiment. But the wheels of the car of British music did not always run smoothly. There were temperamental backfires and skids. Gardiner, testy, choleric, and accustomed to have his own way, had little experience as a conductor, and in the course of an unwise preliminary address to the orchestra told them so, very politely begging them "to bear with him" and allow for any mistakes he might make. Now orchestral players in those far-off pre-B.B.C. days were for the most part "toughs," very much more unregimented than the docile ranks of Broadcasting House, and the "N.S.O.," indifferent or positively hostile to nearly all this new music, and taking advantage of their conductor's alternating diffidence and uncontrolled outbursts of irritation, behaved at times like a herd of sulky schoolboys.

Matters were not improved when late at one afternoon rehearsal a lady in the chorus rose on her stalwart hind legs and, in a voice shaking with temper, charged the players with scamping their job. "We in the choir have put our hearts into our work," she shouted, "and we think it is up to you at least to take some interest and not let us down!"

One morning during the second series Balfour was to meet me after rehearsal for lunch at Pagani's. He kept me waiting—an ominous sign—for usually he was as punctual as the sun, and when he did turn up his face was red as a turkey's crop and his blue eyes were ablaze. "I am sorry, Arnold," he burst out, puffing slightly, "that you will not hear 'In the Faery Hills' to-night, but the concert is off!" He made a furious gesture with both arms. "Those people are simply intolerable! I have told the manager that I'll pay in full, but I'll have no more to do with them. Never again! Never!" Somehow or other appeasement was effected during the next few hours—possibly through Norman O'Neill's influence—and the concert took place after all. But he had meant it when he said he had had enough, and at the close of the 1913 series he discontinued his venture. He may have been chagrined and disillusioned himself, but Vaughan Williams, Holst, Percy Grainger, and I owed him a debt of gratitude impossible to repay.

He had saved Holst from neglect and a weighty sense of personal failure, and had fairly launched me on my orchestral career.

In the spring of 1914 his Maecenas role was assumed by a newcomer, Bevis Ellis, one of the De Walden family, a charming young man-about-town and an amateur of all the arts. Ellis also drew up several programmes, one of them of chamber music, but, since experience had proved that public and critics alike were apt to look upon an all-British concert as a kind of raree-show outside the main trend of the art, he deemed it wiser to leaven native music with little-known works by established foreign masters.

One of his concerts was made ever memorable by the first performance (under Geoffrey Toye) of Ralph Vaughan Williams's "London" Symphony, in its original form and longer and more diffuse than the well-knit composition we now know. The symphony has been no doubt improved, though I personally regret the loss of a mysterious passage of strange and fascinating cacophony with which the first version of the scherzo closed.

At these concerts Geoffrey Toye was given a full chance to establish his reputation as a conductor, although Bevis himself directed a few items and even dared to tackle "Don Quixote" (he idolized Strauss, and I was told with bated breath by George Butterworth that I had the signal honour to be the only member of Ellis's circle allowed to make the least adverse criticism of his deity!).

Bevis, the tactful and urbane, got on well with the orchestral players, who even confessed themselves astonished at his familiarity with every detail of that most elaborate of Richard Strauss's scores.

Dear, eager, intelligent, humorous, half-feminine Bevis Ellis! I became much attached to him during that sinister carnival time, the London summer of 1914, and almost every evening we spent together either at his highly civilized Albany flat or at Covent Garden or some theatre or restaurant. Some might have dismissed him as a dilettante and amateur of life and art, but if that be granted he was surely an amateur of a very rare kind. I have never met anyone whose methods were so thorough, and he would fling the full energy of his mind into any pursuit he took up. Just as his inside knowledge of "Don Quixote" had startled the orchestra, so when he reluctantly but resolutely took up soldiering (a calling for which by temperament he could have had no sort of bent) he determined that he would master his subject from top to bottom, from A to Z. The last time I saw him he was wearing the red and gold tabs of a staff officer.

In the middle of the war I received a signed photograph of him from his sister. There was no letter of explanation, but I guessed the worst. He had been killed by an explosion in the trenches somewhere in France, and no trace of his body was ever found.

I was with him in Cornwall for a few days just after the outbreak of war and he was, I realized, in the throes of indecision about joining up, but his reserve kept his mouth shut tight as a clam. One morning I came downstairs to find that he had gone back to town and the recruiting office without a word of farewell.

I often wonder whether during that lonely and silent conflict within him he had any premonition of his end.

"Æ" AND OTHERS

By 1911 I was married, and at last able to realize a long-cherished dream of actually setting up house in Ireland. For two winters I rented a furnished villa in Bushy Park Road, Rathgar, Co. Dublin. That was the correct postal address, and those two small letters before the name of the city held for me a certain poetry, hinting as they did at green fields and the hills. Nor was this an idle fancy, for from the back windows of the incongruously named "Yeovil" there was, a quarter of a century ago, a clear vista of parklike wooded country and beyond that of the complete ring of the untamed

Dublin Mountains. On any clear day one's eye could wander along
that amphitheatre of beloved slopes, over Niall Glundubh's cairn
on Tibradden, past haunted Kilmashogue, down into the sylvan
hollows of Glendhu, up again along a red-brown fringe of leafless
trees to the sinister ruins of Kilikee brooding over Dublin's south-
western suburbs—"the Hellfire Club," monumental to the arrogance and violence of the eighteenth-century Irish gentry—until
finally one's gaze rested upon Seefin, a pearl-grey phantasm of a
mountain, its summit gleaming maybe with the snowdrifts of last
week's blizzard. And deep in those folded hills, thirty miles away,
was hidden Glendalough of the Seven Churches, an enchanted place
of holy gloom.

No sooner was I settled in than Clifford was invited to stay with
me. He had known George Russell ("Æ") for some years, and we
lost no time in going round the corner to 17 Rathgar Avenue that
I might be introduced to the poet whose work I had always
revered (revered for its spiritual content but hardly admired) for
"Æ's" technical skill in verse was little better than that conspicuously lacking in his painting. He had small rhythmical invention and
weak lines were inclined to mar even his loveliest poems.

We were warmly welcomed, and whilst I prowled round the
walls of the studio examining iridescent pictures of children playing
or dancing by the sea's edge, or strange delineations of the *sidhe*,
the fairies and elementals that Russell professed sometimes to see, I
listened for the first time to one of those mellifluous if often almost
incoherent rhapsodical monologues concerning the "Gawds" and
the eternities that heard once or twice were so spell-binding, and
later, after many repetitions, became even tiresome.

Monologues is certainly the word, for "Æ" could not converse,
and, if one dared to intrude a remark, had an irritating habit of
shouting "What's that? What's that?" though he had heard
perfectly well what you had said.

The pictures enthralling me, and finding myself a little out of my
depth in the ethereal mists of that rarefied discourse, I was so silent
that at last even my host noticed it and asked if I were perhaps not
interested in the adventures of the soul. On my assuring him that I
thought there was little else worthy of sustained consideration he
looked quite relieved and instantly invited me to come again with

my brother next Sunday. It was his way to leave his front door ajar every Sunday evening when he and his wife kept open house to his friends and any friends of theirs they might like to bring along.

"Æ" called the years from 1912 to 1914 "Dublin's Golden Age," and in that studio in the course of two or three visits I met nearly all the writers and artists with whom I was to become intimate during the coming winter.

Padraic Colum was always there, of course, with his noble profile and tiny body, ever alert as a robin-redbreast. Everything seemed to interest him. As someone remarked, "Colum absorbs knowledge not only with his ears and brain, but through every pore of his skin!" The friendliest soul on earth was Padraic, and the purest and most generous nature I ever had the good luck to encounter. To hear a malicious word about anyone, even though thoroughly deserved, was positive pain to him, and he should have served as a perpetual reproof to tattling Dublin, where "the acoustics have always been so perfect." Molly, his brilliant wife, with her dagger-like witty and learned brain, could look for a moment more beautiful than any woman I have ever seen. She had no features to boast of but the most glorious cloud of red-gold hair, and when this was loose (it was very fine and always quite uncontrollable) and her hazel-green eyes, wild with some mental excitement, gleaming through its shining mesh, she might have been a radiant young visitant from another world.

Pale of face—a huge domed brow—and scanty untidy black hair, an intellectual leprechaun of a fellow, such was James Stephens, soon to become famous in a day with *The Crock of Gold*. He had already published several things, among them *The Charwoman's Daughter* and an interesting and individual book of verse, *The Hill of Vision*.

There was a certain amount of rather wild religious speculation in some of these poems, and as we sauntered by the banks of the Dodder one evening "Æ" remarked to me, "I think Stephens is a little too free with Gawd (God). His attitude is rather like that of an African heathen towards his joss. When things are not going well with our friend he bangs God about and pitches him into the corner amongst the rubbish. And then an hour later, feeling some compunction at the forlorn appearance of the old fellow, he sets God up again and seeks to propitiate him with libation and sacrifice."

Stephens was soon my friend, as also was Ernest Boyd, an argumentative but affectionate collector of first editions of modern Anglo-Irish literature and its earliest historian. He had a magnificently deep measured speech, its rich vibrations making vases and glasses in any room in which he was speaking rattle and ring (or very nearly, if you must have it so!). He had a cold clear brain, and when in full spate was capable of overwhelming by sheer weight of sound any but the most seasoned opponent.

Always an attractively curious and eager member of the coterie was a chic and pretty French girl, teacher of her own tongue in Dublin, and much mistrusted by most of the younger married women, though there was no reason in this, for Madeleine Regnier was in reality a simple and warm-hearted little person, ready to make friends with everyone she met, irrespective of sex. One fancied that had she been a dog she would never have ceased wagging her tail.

And there were two conscientiously Celtic ladies, always draped sentimentally in silken robes of what they supposed to be ancient Irish model and design. (Russell once astonishingly said, "Whenever I read any verse by either of those two, I always feel an inordinate desire for the public-house!") One of them at least was of unmixed English birth, and later, marrying another Sassenach, brought up her children to speak Irish and nothing else, whilst her husband (who hailed from Lancashire) was wont to stand in the corridor of the Dublin to Galway express, refusing to budge for any fellow-passenger on the way to the lavatory who requested him in English to be allowed to pass. But there came a day when "Æ," for once irritated out of his Olympian calm, frankly told him that it was damned bad manners to talk to other people in a language of which they knew nothing.

These were all regular weekly visitors to Rathgar Avenue, but there were many others who would drift in occasionally, amongst them Seamus O'Sullivan, sombrely handsome and a subtle, crepuscular poet. His appearance brought to mind a comparison with a noble funeral horse.

Very infrequent guests were T. H. Kelleher (an Irish H. V.

G

Morton) and Thomas McDonagh, doomed to execution after the 1916 rising, just as, in Yeats's phrase, "he was coming into his force" as a poet.

And lastly Con Marcievicz would now and again rush in just as everyone was about to leave, nerves all a-jangle, limbs never still. and her words tripping over one another in her slightly gasping speech. An ill-balanced, politically intolerant woman, but with a heart of gold for everyone but Tommies, the Dublin Metropolitan Police, and the R.I.C. She and Maud Gonne were alike adored by the Dublin poor.

But Yeats (or Yeets as "Æ" invariably pronounced the name) was never there, for he and Russell were estranged from one another at that period. The former, although he thought well of Colum and Stephens, had no patience with kindhearted "Æ's" spoon-feeding of fledgling poets, and satirized them in an epigram:

> You say, as I have often given tongue
> In praise of what another's said or sung,
> 'Twere politic to do the like by these,
> But was there ever dog who praised his fleas?

Amongst all these folk "Æ" would squat on the floor, cross-legged in Yogi fashion, and pour forth a continuous stream of divine babble to the enthralment of every newcomer. But on these occasions Mrs. Russell was not happy, knowing all too well that few of the guests took herself much into account, except as a dispenser of tea and cake. Nor did I ever hear the poet himself address a word to her. Stephens once suggested that "Æ's" belief in the immortality of the soul was so assured that, with all eternity before them, he possibly thought it scarcely worth while to pay his wife any special attention at Rathgar, Co. Dublin, in 1912!

DERMOT O'BYRNE

I had begun to write short stories—always upon Irish subjects—in 1909, and two of these Clifford had printed in one of a series of booklets associated with his now long-dead art magazine *Orpheus*.

This little volume, published under the pseudonym of Dermot O'Byrne, consisted of two stories, "The Sisters" and "Green

Magic," dedicated to "Æ", and soon after I was settled in Rathgar and beginning to be intimate with the poet-painter, I aroused all my courage and diffidently presented him with a copy. To my delight he was quite enthusiastic about these tales and spoke of them to many in his Sunday circle, including Padraic and Molly Colum and Ernest Boyd. (If he liked anything one had written he would rush round at once with charmingly simple impetuosity to tell one so.)

At that time Colum was editor of the *Irish Review*, a monthly magazine (oddly enough in Dublin) devoted more especially to literary matters than to politics, and in this paper he printed a short play of mine called "On the Hill," and a wild and semi-humorous yarn of the Donegal tinkers.

By degrees I accumulated more than enough material for a full-sized book, and *Children of the Hills* was brought out by Messrs. Maunsel, to be followed by *Wrack*, recommended to the Talbot Press by Ernest Boyd, then the firm's reader.

These collections found favour with many of my Dublin friends, with "Æ" and the Colums particularly enthusiastic, and their pleasure in this sideline of my invention was a pure joy to me; for I was still in my first innocence and bewilderment as a recognized literary figure in the city, and was thrilled with pride to be accounted one of those

> Who sang to lighten Ireland's wrong
> Ballad and story, rann and song.

My allegiance in those years was divided between literature and music. I wrote most of my stories in the remotest regions of the west, very often in the very place where the scene of my tale was set, and devoted the major part of my time in Dublin to composition, though I spoke little of music to my Irish associates. In later years "Æ", whenever he met me or my name came up, could always be counted upon to declare that the whole time I lived in Dublin he was totally unaware that I was a musician at all. This was not strictly true, but he enjoyed repeating his little anecdote *ad nauseam*.

DUBLIN EVENINGS

Some of us followed "Æ's" example in keeping open house one evening in the week, and thus one met one's friends almost every day. I remember that James Stephens entertained on Mondays, the Colums on Tuesday, myself on Wednesday, whilst every Thursday night we breathed purest *urkeltisch* air at the house of the two Druid priestesses aforementioned.

I should think that more than half of those long-silenced discussions must have been concerned with Ireland from some aspect or other, for, as in Russia and Poland, the shadow of the nation broods over all gatherings of Irish folk, and the voice of the dark land beyond the window-panes mingles sooner or later in every conversation.

New friends and acquaintances were gradually added to the list of those I had originally met in Rathgar Avenue; the O'Rahilly, a strikingly handsome young man, always dressed in a saffron kilt, who was destined to be killed in O'Connell Street during Easter Week; Professor Rudmose Brown, half-Danish, an inquiring, fatly genial man with a vast pink-and-white face that somehow made you want to laugh; John Eglinton (George Moore's "contrary John"), curator of the National Library and author of several little books of astute criticism written in a scrupulously fastidious style. John would stand no nonsense from Irish-Irelanders, Gaelic language fanatics, or any sort of "sentimentalist," and spoke shockingly of Cathleen ní Hoolihan as a "bedraggled beldam with holy water on her brow and whisky on her breath," but somehow he was universally liked and respected.

One day in midwinter Colum returned from Achill, eager and enthusiastic as ever. "I've been staying with Darrell Figgis," he cried breathlessly, "and had a great time. He's tremendously keen on your *Children of the Hills*, Arnold. 'Who is this Dermot O'Byrne?' says he, and when I told him I knew you well, 'I must meet that man,' says Darrell. 'Tell him to come over here any time he likes and stay a week.'"

"Do you think he meant it?" said I.

"He did surely. Send him a wire to-day to say you're coming."

This I did, and next evening found myself in Keel above the amethyst caves and the green Atlantic.

Little did I dream then that within a few years both host and hostess would be dead by their own hands.

Darrell was an attractive-looking fellow ("a mixture of Synge and a renaissance prince" was Colum's flattering portrait) but he was woefully unstable and vain. He showed a handsome façade, but there was little behind it and he was never really in favour with, or in the confidence of, his fellow-rebels, who nicknamed him "the man from Golders Green" (he had lived in England for years before he took up with the Irish republican movement). His literary work was negligible, both as novelist and poet, and he published a short book (a kind of oblation) upon "Æ" and his art which was a source of some embarrassment to its subject.

His tragic wife had a far deeper nature and a more reliable character.

As time passed and 1913 was drawing to a close there were underground mutterings in Dublin, whispered rumours at street corners, and a gradual increase of tension. Carson had brought off his gun-running coup, and the Ulster Volunteers were known to be arming and drilling purposefully. The movement in the north was countered by the formation of the National Volunteers, in which Colum and others were soon enrolled, and at about the same time Captain Jack White (son of the defender of Ladysmith) started the Citizens' Army, a labour organization for the protection of the workers' interests in the city.

When the order for the Easter Monday rising of 1916 was issued a party of the National Volunteers (by then known as the Irish Republican Army) was detailed off to occupy the roof of Jacob's biscuit factory. No sooner were they there than one of Jack White's Citizens' Army appeared on the scene. After eyeing the newcomer suspiciously for some minutes in silence, the I.R.A. sergeant said coldly, "I suppose you know that this is a Republican Army rebellion?" "Oh," replied the other politely, "I hope I don't intrude!"

In the winter of 1913-14 I was seriously thinking of renting a charming old house outside Rathfarnham on the Bohernabreena road. It had once been the house of either Robert Emmet or his sweetheart, Sarah Curran—I forget which—and I often wonder what dramatic turn my life might have taken, in a place with such associations, had not the war intervened, sending me back to England.

WHITE MAGIC

I was in Glencolumcille in the autumn of 1912 when I received a postcard from "Æ" suggesting that I should join him for a week at Breaghy, near Dunfanaghy, where he went every September to paint. A day or two later I set off on my bicycle for that faraway place at the other side of County Donegal. I toiled over the vast wilderness of high bogland between Glen and Glengesh, led my machine down that truly awful hill, loose stones clattering and tumbling after me, and pedalled into squalid Ardara and thence to Port Noo on the sea-coast. There I came unexpectedly upon a wedding, that of one of the comeliest, gayest, and most affectionate Irish girls I had ever known. I have often thought of you since, Mary Cannon, with your ever laughing eyes and mouth, and have wondered how you fared with your coastguard, and whether he proved worthy of you.

Next day I started again, riding now into the Rosses' country (with at first rather stiff thighs) over those strangely red roads that look as though dyed with ancient carnage and that work an almost hypnotic effect upon the eye and brain. From Burtonport of the granite I took train to Dunfanaghy Road, and thence after picking up my suitcase went on to Breaghy by outside car. There at the door of a snug thatched cottage on a hill and surrounded by whin-bushes I descried "Æ's" burly and bearded form, his kindly short-sighted eyes peering out in search of me. Within the house we were mothered by a simple apple-cheeked old lady, and fed sumptuously on freshly caught salmon, superb eggs, and a huge and monstrously rich home-made cake.

It was an odd entranced week that I spent there, quite dreamlike in the guttering candlelight of memory. Close by our hillock were the fine house and estate of Sir Hugh Law, a Nationalist M.P. who, an old friend of "Æ", had loaned him a summer house in the wooded grounds above the sea in which he might paint on wet days.

I have not met with many experiences which cannot be accounted for by a rational explanation, but one of these occurred in that place in the dripping Breaghy woods.

My friend was painting at his easel in the middle of the floor, in his absorption allowing his pipe to go out every two minutes and having to cross to the mantelpiece for a light, so that between the easel and the fireplace there was a track strewn with hundreds of dead matches.

I was reading in the window seat near the door, and we had not spoken for perhaps a quarter of an hour when I suddenly became aware that I was listening to strange sounds, the like of which I had never heard before. They can only be described as a kind of mingling of rippling water and tiny bells tinkled, and yet I could have written them out in ordinary musical notation.

"Do you hear music?" said "Æ" quietly. "I do," I replied, and even as I spoke utter silence fell. I do not know what it was we both heard that morning and must be content to leave it at that.

Even in Tirconaill it is not raining all the time, and there were enchanted twilights on the strand with Lomair, a great Irish wolf-hound of Sir Hugh's, tearing about in the shadows and leaping incredible heights over bushes and walls. He might have been one of the ghostly giant hounds of ancient heroic lore.

As the dusk deepened many-coloured lights tossed and flickered along the ridges of the mountains. "Don't you wish you were amongst them?" murmured my companion, and I knew he meant that we were gazing upon the host of fairy. Even under the spell of that lovely hour and with an intense will to believe it seemed to me more probable that those dancing shapes of flame were something to do with the retinae of my own eyes straining into the semi-darkness, and no far-off reality, and "Æ" was asked whether his visions of elementals and the *sidhe* were subjective or the reverse. To this he returned a somewhat evasive answer, saying that he thought both at different times, and I could never decide whether his famous clairvoyance was mere romantic make-believe and deception of himself and others, or whether he in truth beheld those mighty iris-hued forms invisible to ordinary men.

During that week he made me try to concentrate on certain elemental ideas and to discover their associating images. "Think of the sea and do your best to exclude every other preoccupation. You won't be able to keep it up for more than a few seconds at first, for true concentration is the most arduous exercise the mind of man can attempt. But try, and you may find a visionary symbol suddenly form in the depths of your consciousness.

"I tried to induce Colum, who should be mystically inclined, to experiment when he was here with me last year, but his timid little Catholic soul became afraid. He had some notion, I suppose, that I was inviting him to dabble in black magic!"

Obediently I left him to walk a while by the seashore, and on my return I said, "I saw a white sword in a quivering circle of deep red." "Quite correct." said "Æ", "that was the Druid sword of Mananaan Maclir, the sea-god of the ancient Irish!"

"Perhaps," I ventured, "the test was not so very severe, for I believe that water is my natural element." His "long grey pantheistic eyes" peered at me seriously from behind his spectacles. "Beware of believing any such thing," he cried earnestly, "unless you are certain of it, for water of all the elements is the most dangerous for evil!"

No! I never could quite make "Æ" out, never finally resolve the problem of his sincerity, or fathom how much of the—perhaps unconscious—charlatan there was in his make-up.

From my own observation I should say that he was but a careless and uninterested husband and father (I once overheard him ask Isoult Gonne, "Tell me, what is my boy Dermot like? You must know far more about him than I do!") There can be no doubt that he had at least a streak of vanity, and the easy adoration of American women's clubs must have been as meat and drink to him; but on the other hand he always conveyed an impression of intense personal conviction even in his most cloudy and empyrean flights and most extravagant claims to mystic vision.

Again, was he not an extremely practical agricultural-economist, Sir Horace Plunkett's right-hand man in the I.A.O.S.? and did he not spend a great part of his younger days bicycling all over Ireland, and earnestly and often successfully preaching the advantage of co-operation to the stubborn and conservative peasant mind?

And, above all, does not the best of his verse and prose soar upon rainbow wings of authentic spiritual loveliness? Yet I always doubt those visions, and for me George Russell will ever remain an enigma.

P. H. PEARSE

Molly Colum was always eager for me to meet Padraig Pearse, the principal of St. Enda's College, Rathfarnham, where his curious aim was to teach Irish children to be Irish, to speak the native language, and to learn the true history of their own land. This school was doing very well up to 1916, and then . . . But we all know that "unpractical" visionary's end.

Molly had an admiration for him only little less than that she felt for W. B. Yeats.

"You *must* meet him, Arnold! Sure you would get on together like sworn brothers, but the trouble is he's a very difficult fish to land. He always refuses to go to any sort of party. However, I'll try." On one of my Wednesday evenings a week or two later Molly entered excitedly with that queer flame in her eyes that gave her the semblance of a woman of the other world. "Listen, Arnold," she cried, "I have made Pearse promise to come here this very evening. I may tell you I pitched it in strong about your charms, and it's a triumph for both you and me!"

Pearse arrived soon after, and scarcely had he shaken hands shyly and gravely with myself, my wife, and the few guests present than he sat down by the fire with his face in his hands and stared into the blaze as though absorbed in a private dream. His expression was gentle and even almost womanish, but his eyes were lit with the unwavering flame of the fanatic.

I began to talk to him of his native Connemara which I knew well, and he became quite animated when I spoke in lively detail of places on that ultimate seaboard that it is unlikely that anyone else in the room had ever heard of. Said Molly by my side, "My goodness, Mr. Pearse, would you ever have supposed that this fella' was an Englishman?" "Well," replied Pearse quietly, with the ghost of an ironic smile, "I'm half-English myself!"

Presently, his attention being engaged by someone else, Molly half-whispered, "Pearse wants to die for Ireland, you know. It has been the ideal of his whole life."

Indeed he did not have much longer to wait before his desire was granted.

As he was leaving that night he said to Molly, "I think your friend Arnold Bax may be one of us. I should like to see more of him." I was anxious to meet him again too, but somehow it chanced that I never did. I could not forget the impression that strange death-aspiring dreamer made upon me, and when on Easter Tuesday 1916 I read by Windermere's shore of that wild, scatter-brained, but burningly idealist adventure in Dublin the day before, I murmured to myself, "I *know* that Pearse is in this!"

VIGNETTE, JUNE 1913

Derrynane, and the summer sunshine pouring down on the little ruinous chapel on a spit of land jutting out into the Kenmare River. By its side an ancient untidy cemetery, choked with coarse grasses and weeds. Some humble Kerry peasant has just been buried; the mourners are dispersing slowly; but two shawled women remain behind. Without a word or a glance between them they drop to their knees, facing one another at each end of a grave—a mere coffin-shaped mound of earth—and squatting on their heels, staring now into each other's eyes, rock backwards and forwards howling antiphonally. This pagan keening, old as the soil of Ireland, sounds less human than the screeching of the gulls wheeling above the women's heads in the bright air.

SPRING IN CO. DUBLIN AND FAREWELL, MY YOUTH

Irritably I tapped my pencil upon the sheet of manuscript paper, scribbled an almost illegible bar; and then, tilting back my chair and biting deep dents in the end of the pencil, stared at the dazzle of parallel black lines on the white paper before me.

This damned thing would not go at all this morning, and yet only last night after a hard smooth day's work I had gone exulting to bed, believing that I was to make something really fine out of my material. Rousing myself with a jerk I planted the sheet angrily upon the piano-desk and ran over the few bars I had contrived since I had set to work after breakfast, seeking desperately for a logical continuation. Nothing sensible came of it, and with an impatient exclamation I struck a few hideous discords, leaving my foot on the pedal, so that the jangled sounds throbbed and roared from the depths of the huge upright Bechstein. "No good trying to-day," I muttered, allowing my mind to empty itself to a dismal void. I touched my burning temples with chilly fingertips, staring at the glare of the white paper on the desk until the black staves upon it swam into strange warped shapes, edged with red and yellow, before my smarting eyes. Rubbing them hard with my knuckles and lolling moodily to the window, I found my attention unconsciously drawn to a small protuberance at the end of a branch out there on a level with the sill. I threw up the sash and the soft air of a late March morning stole into the room. Yes! there was no doubt about it, the perfect little cup of brown and silky white was breaking. Inside I could already see the shy tender pink of the first blooming of the world of trees.

Spring, by Jove! Why should I torment myself indoors on such a day? I would hunt out my bicycle and make for the hills.

Under a cool flecked sky I rode out, taking the road over the Dodder bridge, the moss about its bastions the softest and greenest in the world—past one of the greatest strongholds of the Pale against the forays of the Irishry from the Wicklow Mountains—its noble park now being ravaged by jerry-builders—and on through Rathfarnham, noteworthy for the amazing fecundity of its women and its air of an old and lonely country village, so convincing that the grinding approach of the Drumcondra tram always brought with it a sense of illusion. (Last April I was there again after a year or two's absence, and my eyes were affronted by the gaudiest and most vulgar petrol station I ever saw, completely blocking out the once picturesque view up the main street of Kilikee and the Hellfire Club.)

Here the direct influence of the city was left behind and I followed the windings of a very muddy road between high stone walls, overtopped by ancient trees. I passed several squalid hamlets on the left side of the road, whilst on the right the monotony of the wall was occasionally varied by a massive gateway through which I caught a glimpse of a long double drive circling a plot of ill-kept grass, and leading with a pathetic pretence of pomp to a flight of steps climbing to the elevated front door of a small country house dating from the eighteenth century—its façade washed over in peeling plaster of pink or cream or chalk-blue.

By the time I had left the outskirts of Rathfarnham the sudden quickening of the season was beginning to excite me deliciously. Looking up at the trees as I passed beneath them I could see that every tiny bud was swollen almost to bursting point; indeed one or two almonds had already flung out their delicate glory, and the mosses and lichens on the old damp walls bordering the road seemed veiled in a suffused film of deeper and softer green—a kind of liquescence of light.

The new tenderness in the air enveloped me capriciously, touching my cheek like a girl's first shy kiss and with almost the same effect of something pathetically unsullied.

In my mind sang uninvoked fragments of an old composition of mine—a work inspired by this very wistfulness in the presence of newly born spring. My heart exulted. "Well, I did it that time!" I said to myself, my eye on a squirrel bobbing across the road close to my wheel, "I must be the devil of a fellow after all!"

I had escaped now from the companionship of those uncompromising stone walls, and, entering an open country of low hedges and embankments and wide stretching meadowlands, began to feel definitely the longed-for sense of the mountains, clear to view by this time and swiftly closing in upon me.

I gazed with a new delight at the deciduous slated and thatched cabins, crumbled bridges, low ruinous walls, and especially the old estates and manor houses of the gentry, as though all these homely things had been roused into refreshed life with the season. Always to my mind these old dwellings in their snug decay possessed a certain dingy dignity, suggesting some great-great-grandfather of Grattan's day, shabbily refined of attire, short in the purse, but of recognized integrity, and now fallen asleep, snuff-box in hand after finishing the very last bottle of ancestral port from the cellar. These ancient buildings sunk in unruffled lethargy seemed wonderfully self-sufficient. Surely even to-day their great-paned sombre windows must fail to mirror any shadow of motor-cars and telegraph-poles to the ghosts of daredevil eighteenth-century gallantry that unquestionably lingered in many of their damp and dark interiors. Even the disreputable ruin on Kilikee, popularly associated with flagrant outrages and abominable Satan-worshipping orgies—a wind-whipped place of desolation that even by daylight I could never approach without a slight shudder—seemed, bathed now in the mellow gleam of that still March noon, to have attained an affectation of decency, like a plausible rogue assuming the manners of respectable neighbours.

The thought struck me more forcibly than ever before that for a whole century and a half this corner of the earth had evaded the eye of progress. It was still late eighteenth century in County Dublin, as in many parts even of the city itself. And now it was all too old and sleepy to awaken again in the ordinary course of human affairs. Only a cataclysm could ever disturb its drowsy retrospective dream of bewigged and embroidered violence and lechery, of priest-baiting and faction-fighting, of a starved unlettered peasantry, shrewd and metaphorical of speech, of the flaming follies and heroisms of scatter-brained yet noble revolt against alien tyranny.

Meanwhile the closely fleeced sky was lightening, sifted by some lively wind too high to touch earth. Soft clouds formed, pooled in pale golden spaces, and amongst them the phantom disc of the sun showed for an instant, heralding the coming clearing of the atmosphere. The whole world stirred out of sleep.

Passing over a small bridge at the foot of the hill that climbs through the woods of Glendhu I dismounted, and whilst pushing the machine energetically up the steep slope I thought of that excitable man who had once said that in Ireland we are unable to enjoy the spring. "I suppose I must be wholly English to-day," I murmured to myself.

In the deep silence of the Glendhu wood, a stillness only broken by the sound of the brook tumbling through the glen from the hills, the pent energy of the season seemed so tensely leashed that I felt the boughs and roots might at any moment become vocal—a songful burgeoning of bud and leaf.

At the cross-roads I paused, leaning on the parapet of the old bridge. I held my breath and listened, staring through the bare trees at the blue dimness of distance where the horizon of the great midland plain was lifted half up the sky. I could hear nothing but the pounding of my pulse and the tinkle of the little stream over the stones.

And then a strange thing happened. Once or twice before in the last few years something similar had occurred to me—always when I had been alone.

Whilst my vision became saturated with that aerial colour of Irish distances the two sounds of which I was alone aware were in a moment fused into one. My life's blood it was that laughed and danced down the mountain, and the hill-stream coursed through my veins—was my very being. I was also that blue rim of earth held in the tangled net of the still naked birch-stems, and deep in that multicoloured pool of consciousness I sensed the images of all the beauty and pain in beauty that had ever illuminated or shadowed the race-memory of man.

It only lasted for a moment. "Who am I? Where am I?" came the question in a kind of panic, and instantly the dusky flames in that mirror within me broke up into shafts of diminishing light and went out altogether. My consciousness slid back into the rather delicate physical organism that was known as Arnold Bax. At the same moment I was made acutely aware of the soreness of an elbow, pressed hard against the crumbled stone of the bridge-parapet.

I took a deep breath and went on up the hill. I had no understanding of these rapt moments, in retrospect so impalpable and obscure. They always came quite unexpectedly. I remembered the last time. It had happened in a wood somewhere in the south of England during a frivolous picnic with some young people who shared none of my ideas. Feeling bored, I had strayed away for a few minutes from the rather vulgar artificial and covert flirtations of my companions, with the thought even at the time that my attitude towards them was a bit priggish. Suddenly my eye had become arrested by a young silver birch-tree immediately in my path. It was in no way specially remarkable from many another tree in that wood, yet instantly and without warning a like wonder had snatched me away for one tranced second of time.

Among the pines at the top of the hill I remounted and flew down to Glencullen on a free wheel. Here in these high places the atmosphere was clearer than in the valleys, and as I rode with the cool breeze from the Irish Sea in my teeth down that lonely and surprising glen—where only an extreme alertness of the topographical sense can stay the stranger from believing himself in some mountainy corner of Connaught or Donegal—the sunlight streamed down from a rift in the dispersing clouds, livening the shaking dewdrops and cobwebs on the brown sprays of heather to a tremulousness of rainbow and jewelled light.

Grey-blue wreaths of turf-smoke hung over every cabin, drifting away to the west and dissolving slowly in the quivering violence of the sun's rays. I noticed a solitary farmer idly steering a few sheep in an intricate course among the picturesque insanitary jumble of more or less thatched cottages just below the road—the man and his clothes looking in the strong light no less grey than the beasts, and they too showing but a slight variation of tone from those of the cabins and the scattered rocks of which these higgledy-piggledy buildings seemed projections.

"The perfect assimilation of man to his environment," I reflected admiringly.

I rushed down a short steep descent and then, turning to the left at right angles, pushed my machine uphill again for a quarter of a mile and so fast that I was breathless once more by the time I reached the top.

It was on this height, my face to the blue dazzle of Dublin Bay, the fantastic Three Rock Mountain on the right, and southward Slieve Cullen—in spite of the bathos of its modern name, still one of the noblest of Irish hills—that the climax of the music of that March day should have broken out around me. But as I stood there, panting for breath, a sombre cloud shrouded the sun, a sudden chill air came from the east, and I shivered. Reluctantly I discovered that the careless magic of the day was gone. The wind grew colder and something warned me to delay there no longer. Soberly I rode down the long seaward hill back to town. What was amiss? Had I a premonition of the world tragedy looming on the horizon of a near future? Or did I sense the imminence of a more personal sorrow?

For a day or so later I crossed over to England, not to revisit Ireland for over four years, and with the exception of "Æ" never again to see one of my Dublin friends in the land of Ireland. The golden age was past!

At the outbreak of war, or soon after, the Colums went to America, no more to come back to their native country unless as passing visitors; Ernest Boyd and Madeleine (by now his wife) followed; Stephens gave up his post as curator of the National Gallery of Ireland to work as a literary reviewer on London papers; Pearse and MacDonagh were shot after Easter Week, whilst even the conscientiously Celtic ladies broke up their joint household and departed elsewhere. If I return now I am an utter stranger in that city of my young manhood, knowing amongst its indifferent population not one soul (now that "Æ" too is no more) that was intimate with mine when for too short a time I was an adopted— and, I like to believe, not unloved-child of Eire.

Farewell, my youth!